Dependency Parsing

Synthesis Lectures on Human Language Technologies

Editor

Graeme Hirst, *University of Toronto*

Synthesis Lectures on Human Language Technologies publishes monographs on topics relating to natural language processing, computational linguistics, information retrieval, and spoken language understanding. Emphasis is placed on important new techniques, on new applications, and on topics that combine two or more HLT subfields.

Dependency Parsing

Sandra Kübler, Ryan McDonald, and Joakim Nivre
2009

Statistical Language Models for Information Retrieval

ChengXiang Zhai
2009

Dependency Parsing

Sandra Kübler, Ryan McDonald, and Joakim Nivre

ISBN: 978-3-031-01003-3   paperback
ISBN: 978-3-031-02131-2   ebook

DOI 10.1007/978-3-031-02131-2

A Publication in the Springer Nature series
SYNTHESIS LECTURES ON HUMAN LANGUAGE TECHNOLOGIES

Lecture #2
Series Editor: Graeme Hirst, *University of Toronto*

Series ISSN
Synthesis Lectures on Human Language Technologies
ISSN pending.

Dependency Parsing

Sandra Kübler
Department of Linguistics, Indiana University

Ryan McDonald
Google Research

Joakim Nivre
Department of Linguistics and Philology, Uppsala University
School of Mathematics and System Engineering, Växjö University

SYNTHESIS LECTURES ON HUMAN LANGUAGE TECHNOLOGIES #2

ABSTRACT

Dependency-based methods for syntactic parsing have become increasingly popular in natural language processing in recent years. This book gives a thorough introduction to the methods that are most widely used today. After an introduction to dependency grammar and dependency parsing, followed by a formal characterization of the dependency parsing problem, the book surveys the three major classes of parsing models that are in current use: transition-based, graph-based, and grammar-based models. It continues with a chapter on evaluation and one on the comparison of different methods, and it closes with a few words on current trends and future prospects of dependency parsing. The book presupposes a knowledge of basic concepts in linguistics and computer science, as well as some knowledge of parsing methods for constituency-based representations.

KEYWORDS

parsing, syntax, dependency parsing, dependency grammar

Contents

Preface

Dependency-based methods for syntactic parsing have become increasingly popular in natural language processing in recent years. One of the reasons for their success is that they have been shown to work reliably for a wide range of typologically different languages. The increased interest in dependency-based parsing has led to investigations into a range of different parsing algorithms.

The aim of this book is to give readers new to this field an introduction to the parsing algorithms used in dependency parsing. The aim is not to propose new methods or new findings nor to promote a single algorithm but rather to give an overview of existing algorithms and a comparison of their major similarities and differences. Additionally, we will touch upon matters of evaluation and data representation.

This book is aimed at graduate students and researchers in computer science, linguistics, and computational linguistics. It expects familiarity with basic concepts in linguistics and computer science, as well as some knowledge of parsing methods for constituency-based representations. Thus, we expect the reader to be familiar with basic chart parsing algorithms such as the Cocke-Kasami-Younger algorithm or Earley's algorithm. Additionally, we expect the reader to be familiar with the basic concepts of probability theory.

It is helpful, but not necessary, for the reader to be familiar with concepts from machine learning. The book concentrates on supervised approaches to dependency parsing, which rely on a range of different learning approaches: memory-based learning, support vector machines, and perceptron learning, to name just a few. However, these approaches are not central to the understanding of the dependency parsing algorithms.

The book is partly based on material from two courses: The ACL/COLING 2006 tutorial on *Dependency Parsing*, presented by Sandra and Joakim, and the ESSLLI 2007 introductory course *Introduction to Data-Driven Dependency Parsing*, given by Ryan and Joakim. Other material is derived from earlier publications, and we are grateful to the Association for Computational Linguistics for giving us permission to reuse material previously published in various conference proceedings. We also want to thank our co-authors in those publications: Atanas Chanev, Koby Crammer, Gülşen Eryiğit, Jan Hajič, Johan Hall, Kevin Lerman, Svetoslav Marinov, Erwin Marsi, Jens Nilsson, Fernando Pereira, Kiril Ribarov, Sebastian Riedel, Giorgio Satta, Mario Scholz, and Deniz Yuret. In addition, we have drawn on our experience from teaching dependency parsing in courses on computational linguistics and parsing, and we are grateful to all the students who attended these classes, and whose questions and comments helped shape the material presented here.

We owe a special debt to the organizers of the 2006 CoNLL Shared Task, Sabine Buchholz, Amit Dubey, Yuwal Krymolowski, and Erwin Marsi, who set the stage for many of the recent developments in dependency parsing by creating a common platform for research and evaluation.

Finally, we want to thank Gerald Penn, Marco Kuhlmann, and Liu Haitao, who read the first complete draft of the book and suggested numerous improvements. All remaining errors, however, are our own responsibility. We hope you enjoy the book.

Sandra Kübler, Ryan McDonald, and Joakim Nivre
Bloomington, New York City, and Uppsala
December 2008

CHAPTER 1

Introduction

Dependency parsing is an approach to automatic syntactic analysis of natural language inspired by the theoretical linguistic tradition of dependency grammar. After playing a rather marginal role in natural language processing for many years, dependency parsing has recently attracted considerable interest from researchers and developers in the field. One reason for the increasing popularity is the fact that dependency-based syntactic representations seem to be useful in many applications of language technology, such as machine translation and information extraction, thanks to their transparent encoding of predicate-argument structure. Another reason is the perception that dependency grammar is better suited than phrase structure grammar for languages with free or flexible word order, making it possible to analyze typologically diverse languages within a common framework. But perhaps the most important reason is that this approach has led to the development of accurate syntactic parsers for a number of languages, particularly in combination with machine learning from syntactically annotated corpora, or treebanks. It is the parsing methods used by these systems that constitute the topic of this book.

It is important to note from the outset that this is a book about dependency parsing, not about dependency grammar, and that we will in fact have very little to say about the way in which dependency grammar can be used to analyze the syntax of a given natural language. We will simply assume that such an analysis exists and that we want to build a parser that can implement it to automatically analyze new sentences. In this introductory chapter, however, we will start by giving a brief introduction to dependency grammar, focusing on basic notions rather than details of linguistic analysis. With this background, we will then define the task of dependency parsing and introduce the most important methods that are used in the field, methods that will be covered in depth in later chapters. We conclude, as in every chapter, with a summary and some suggestions for further reading.

1.1 DEPENDENCY GRAMMAR

Dependency grammar is rooted in a long tradition, possibly going back all the way to Pāṇini's grammar of Sanskrit several centuries before the Common Era, and has largely developed as a form for syntactic representation used by traditional grammarians, in particular in Europe, and especially for Classical and Slavic languages. The starting point of the modern theoretical tradition of dependency grammar is usually taken to be the work of the French linguist Lucien Tesnière, published posthumously in the late 1950s. Since then, a number of different dependency grammar frameworks have been proposed, of which the most well-known are probably the Prague School's Functional Generative Description, Mel'čuk's Meaning-Text Theory, and Hudson's Word Grammar.

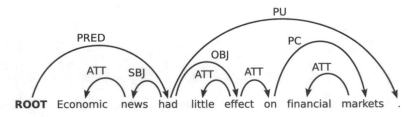

Figure 1.1: Dependency structure for an English sentence.

The basic assumption underlying all varieties of dependency grammar is the idea that syntactic structure essentially consists of *words* linked by binary, asymmetrical relations called *dependency relations* (or *dependencies* for short). A dependency relation holds between a syntactically subordinate word, called the *dependent*, and another word on which it depends, called the *head*.[1] This is illustrated in figure 1.1, which shows a dependency structure for a simple English sentence, where dependency relations are represented by arrows pointing from the head to the dependent.[2] Moreover, each arrow has a label, indicating the *dependency type*. For example, the noun *news* is a dependent of the verb *had* with the dependency type *subject* (SBJ). By contrast, the noun *effect* is a dependent of type *object* (OBJ) with the same head verb *had*. Note also that the noun *news* is itself a syntactic head in relation to the word *Economic*, which stands in the *attribute* (ATT) relation to its head noun.

One peculiarity of the dependency structure in figure 1.1 is that we have inserted an artificial word ROOT before the first word of the sentence. This is a mere technicality, which simplifies both formal definitions and computational implementations. In particular, we can normally assume that every real word of the sentence should have a syntactic head. Thus, instead of saying that the verb *had* lacks a syntactic head, we can say that it is a dependent of the artificial word ROOT. In chapter 2, we will define dependency structures formally as labeled directed graphs, where *nodes* correspond to words (including ROOT) and *labeled arcs* correspond to typed dependency relations.

The information encoded in a dependency structure representation is different from the information captured in a *phrase structure* representation, which is the most widely used type of syntactic representation in both theoretical and computational linguistics. This can be seen by comparing the dependency structure in figure 1.1 to a typical phrase structure representation for the same sentence, shown in figure 1.2. While the dependency structure represents head-dependent relations between *words*, classified by *functional* categories such as subject (SBJ) and object (OBJ), the phrase structure represents the grouping of words into *phrases*, classified by *structural* categories such as noun phrase (NP) and verb phrase (VP).

---

[1]Other terms that are found in the literature are *modifier* or *child*, instead of *dependent*, and *governor*, *regent* or *parent*, instead of *head*. Note that, although we will not use the noun *modifier*, we will use the verb *modify* when convenient and say that a dependent *modifies* its head.

[2]This is the notational convention that we will adopt throughout the book, but the reader should be warned that there is a competing tradition in the literature on dependency grammar according to which arrows point from the dependent to the head.

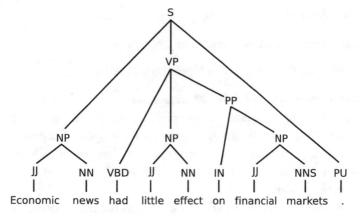

Figure 1.2: Phrase structure for an English sentence.

However, it is important to bear in mind that these differences only concern what is explicitly encoded in the respective representations. For example, phrases can be distinguished in a dependency structure by letting each head word represent a phrase consisting of the word itself and all the words that are dependent on it (possibly in several steps). Conversely, functional relations like subject and object can be identified in a phrase structure in terms of structural configurations (e.g., "NP under S" and "NP under VP"). Nevertheless, practical experience has shown that it is a non-trivial task to perform an automatic conversion from one type of representation to the other (cf. section 6.3). It is also worth noting that many syntactic theories make use of hybrid representations, combining elements of dependency structure with elements of phrase structure. Hence, to describe dependency grammar and phrase structure grammar as two opposite and mutually exclusive approaches to natural language syntax is at best an over-simplification.

If we assume that dependency structure captures an essential element of natural language syntax, then we need some criteria for establishing dependency relations, and for distinguishing the head and the dependent in these relations. Such criteria have been discussed not only in the dependency grammar tradition, but also within other frameworks where the notion of syntactic head plays an important role, including many theories based on phrase structure. Here is a list of some of the more common criteria that have been proposed for identifying a syntactic relation between a head H and a dependent D in a linguistic construction C:[3]

1. H determines the syntactic category of C and can often replace C.

2. H determines the semantic category of C; D gives semantic specification.

3. H is obligatory; D may be optional.

---

[3]The term *construction* is used here in a non-technical sense to refer to any structural complex of linguistic expressions.

4. *H* selects *D* and determines whether *D* is obligatory or optional.

5. The form of *D* depends on *H* (agreement or government).

6. The linear position of *D* is specified with reference to *H*.

It is clear that this list contains a mix of different criteria, some syntactic and some semantic, and one may ask whether there is a single coherent notion of dependency corresponding to all the different criteria. Some theorists therefore posit the existence of several layers of dependency structure, such as morphology, syntax and semantics, or surface syntax and deep syntax. Others have pointed out the need to have different criteria for different kinds of syntactic constructions, in particular for *endocentric* and *exocentric* constructions.

In figure 1.1, the attribute relation (ATT) holding between the noun *markets* and the adjective *financial* is an endocentric construction, where the head can replace the whole without disrupting the syntactic structure:

Economic news had little effect on [financial] markets.

Endocentric constructions may satisfy all of the criteria listed above, although number 4 is usually considered less relevant, since dependents in endocentric constructions are taken to be optional and not selected by their heads. By contrast, the prepositional complement relation (PC) holding between the preposition *on* and the noun *markets* is an exocentric construction, where the head cannot readily replace the whole:

Economic news had little effect on [markets].

Exocentric constructions, by their definition, fail on criterion number 1, at least with respect to substitutability of the head for the whole, but may satisfy the remaining criteria. Considering the rest of the relations exemplified in figure 1.1, the subject and object relations (SBJ, OBJ) are clearly exocentric, and the attribute relation from the noun *news* to the adjective *Economic* clearly endocentric, while the remaining attribute relations (effect → little, effect → on) have a less clear status.

The distinction between endocentric and exocentric constructions is also related to the distinction between *head-complement* and *head-modifier* (or *head-adjunct*) relations found in many contemporary syntactic theories, since head-complement relations are exocentric while head-modifier relations are endocentric. The distinction between complements and modifiers is often defined in terms of *valency*, which is a central notion in the theoretical tradition of dependency grammar. Although the exact characterization of this notion differs from one theoretical framework to the other, valency is usually related to the semantic predicate-argument structure associated with certain classes of lexemes, in particular verbs but sometimes also nouns and adjectives. The idea is that the verb imposes requirements on its syntactic dependents that reflect its interpretation as a semantic predicate. Dependents that correspond to arguments of the predicate can be obligatory or optional in surface syntax but can only occur once with each predicate. By contrast, dependents that do not correspond to arguments can have more than one occurrence with a single predicate and tend to be

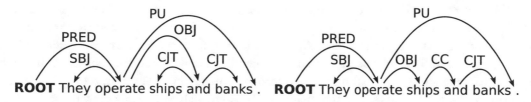

Figure 1.3: Two analyses of coordination in dependency grammar.

optional. The *valency frame* of the verb is normally taken to include argument dependents, but some theories also allow obligatory non-arguments to be included. Returning to figure 1.1, the subject and the object would normally be treated as valency-bound dependents of the verb *had*, while the adjectival modifiers of the nouns *news* and *markets* would be considered valency-free. The prepositional modification of the noun *effect* may or may not be treated as valency-bound, depending on whether the entity undergoing the effect is supposed to be an argument of the noun *effect* or not. Another term that is sometimes used in connection with valency constraints is *arity*, which primarily refers to the *number* of arguments that a predicate takes (without distinguishing the types of these arguments).

While most head-complement and head-modifier structures have a straightforward analysis in dependency grammar, there are also constructions that have a more unclear status. This group includes constructions that involve grammatical function words, such as articles, complementizers and auxiliary verbs, but also structures involving prepositional phrases. For these constructions, there is no general consensus in the tradition of dependency grammar as to whether they should be analyzed as dependency relations at all and, if so, what should be regarded as the head and what should be regarded as the dependent. For example, some theories regard auxiliary verbs as heads taking lexical verbs as dependents; other theories make the opposite assumption; and yet other theories assume that verb chains are connected by relations that are not dependencies in the usual sense.

Another kind of construction that is problematic for dependency grammar (as for most theoretical traditions) is *coordination*. According to the structuralist tradition, coordination is an endocentric construction, since it contains not only one but several heads that can replace the whole construction syntactically. However, this raises the question of whether coordination can be analyzed in terms of binary relations holding between a head and a dependent. Consider the following simple examples:

They operate ships and banks.
She bought and ate an apple.

In the first example, it seems clear that the phrase *ships and banks* functions as a direct object of the verb *operate*, but it is not immediately clear how this phrase can be given an internal analysis that is compatible with the basic assumptions of dependency grammar, since the two nouns *ships* and *banks* seem to be equally good candidates for being heads. Similarly, in the second example, the noun *apple* is the object of the coordinated verb group *bought and ate*, where in some sense both verbs function as the head of the noun. The most popular treatments of coordination in dependency grammar are illustrated for the first example in figure 1.3, where the analysis to the left treats the conjunction as the head, an analysis that may be motivated on semantic grounds, while the analysis on the right treats the conjunction as the head only of the second conjunct and analyzes the conjunction as a dependent of the first conjunct. The arguments for the latter analysis are essentially the same as the arguments for an asymmetric right-branching analysis in phrase structure grammar.

To sum up, the theoretical tradition of dependency grammar is united by the assumption that syntactic structure essentially consists of dependency relations between words. Moreover, there is a core of syntactic constructions for which the analysis given by different frameworks agree in all important respects, notably predicate-argument and head-modifier constructions. However, there are also constructions for which there is no clear consensus, such as verb groups and coordination. Finally, it is worth pointing out that the inventory of dependency types used to classify dependency relations vary from one framework to the other. Besides traditional grammatical functions (such as predicate, subject, and object), semantic roles (such as agent, patient, and goal) are commonly used, especially in representations of deep syntax and semantics. Another dimension of variation is the number of representational levels, or strata, assumed in different theories. Although we will concentrate in this book on mono-stratal representations, using a single dependency structure for syntactic analysis, many theoretical frameworks make use of multi-stratal representations, often with different levels for syntax and semantics.

1.2   DEPENDENCY PARSING

Having introduced the basic notions of dependency grammar, we will now turn to the problem of *dependency parsing*, that is, the task of automatically analyzing the dependency structure of a given input sentence. Throughout this book we will consider a number of different methods for solving this problem, some based on inductive machine learning from large sets of syntactically annotated sentences, others based on formal grammars defining permissible dependency structures. Common to all of these methods is that they do not make any specific assumptions about the kind of dependency types used, be they grammatical functions or semantic roles, nor about the specific analysis of different linguistic constructions, such as verb groups or coordination.

All that is assumed is that the task of the parser is to produce a labeled dependency structure of the kind depicted in figure 1.1, where the words of the sentence (including the artificial word ROOT) are connected by typed dependency relations. This will be made more precise in chapter 2, where we define dependency structures as labeled directed graphs – called *dependency graphs* – and discuss a number of formal properties of these structures. But for the time being we can define the parsing problem as that of mapping an input sentence S, consisting of words $w_0 w_1 \ldots w_n$ (where $w_0 = $ ROOT), to its dependency graph G. In the remainder of this chapter, we will give an overview of the different approaches to this problem that are covered in the book.

Broadly speaking, these approaches can be divided into two classes, which we will call *data-driven* and *grammar-based*, respectively. An approach is data-driven if it makes essential use of *machine learning* from linguistic data in order to parse new sentences. An approach is *grammar-based* if it relies on a *formal grammar*, defining a formal language, so that it makes sense to ask whether a given input sentence is in the language defined by the grammar or not. It is important to note that these categorizations are orthogonal, since it is possible for a parsing method to make essential use of machine learning *and* use a formal grammar, hence to be both data-driven and grammar-based. However, most of the methods that we cover fall into one of these classes only.

The major part of the book, chapters 3–4 to be exact, is devoted to data-driven methods for dependency parsing, which have attracted the most attention in recent years. We focus on *supervised* methods, that is, methods presupposing that the sentences used as input to machine learning have been annotated with their correct dependency structures. In supervised dependency parsing, there are two different problems that need to be solved computationally. The first is the *learning problem*, which is the task of learning a *parsing model* from a representative sample of sentences and their dependency structures. The second is the *parsing problem*, which is the task of applying the learned model to the analysis of a new sentence.[4] We can represent this as follows:

- **Learning:** Given a training set D of sentences (annotated with dependency graphs), induce a parsing model M that can be used to parse new sentences.

- **Parsing:** Given a parsing model M and a sentence S, derive the optimal dependency graph G for S according to M.

Data-driven approaches differ in the type of parsing model adopted, the algorithms used to learn the model from data, and the algorithms used to parse new sentences with the model. In this book, we focus on two classes of data-driven methods, which we call *transition-based* and *graph-based*, respectively. These classes contain most of the methods for data-driven dependency parsing that have been proposed in recent years.

Transition-based methods start by defining a transition system, or state machine, for mapping a sentence to its dependency graph. The learning problem is to induce a model for predicting the next state transition, given the transition history, and the parsing problem is to construct the optimal transition sequence for the input sentence, given the induced model. This is sometimes referred to as shift-reduce dependency parsing, since the overall approach is inspired by deterministic shift-reduce parsing for context-free grammars. Transition-based approaches are treated in chapter 3.

Graph-based methods instead define a space of candidate dependency graphs for a sentence. The learning problem is to induce a model for assigning scores to the candidate dependency graphs for a sentence, and the parsing problem is to find the highest-scoring dependency graph for the input sentence, given the induced model. This is often called maximum spanning tree parsing, since the problem of finding the highest-scoring dependency graph is equivalent, under certain assumptions,

---

[4]The parsing problem is sometimes referred to as the *inference problem* or *decoding problem*, which are the general terms used in machine learning for the application of a learned model to new data.

to the problem of finding a maximum spanning tree in a dense graph. Graph-based approaches are treated in chapter 4.

Most data-driven approaches, whether transition-based or graph-based, assume that any input string is a valid sentence and that the task of the parser is to return the most plausible dependency structure for the input, no matter how unlikely it may be. Grammar-based approaches, by contrast, make use of a formal grammar that only accepts a subset of all possible input strings. Given our previous characterization of the parsing problem, we may say that this formal grammar is an essential component of the model M used to parse new sentences. However, the grammar itself may be hand-crafted or learned from linguistic data, which means that a grammar-based model may or may not be data-driven as well. In chapter 5, we discuss selected grammar-based methods for dependency parsing, dividing them into two classes, which we call *context-free* and *constraint-based*, respectively.

Context-free dependency parsing exploits a mapping from dependency structures to context-free phrase structure representations and reuses parsing algorithms originally developed for context-free grammar. This includes chart parsing algorithms, which are also used in graph-based parsing, as well as shift-reduce type algorithms, which are closely related to the methods used in transition-based parsing.

Constraint-based dependency parsing views parsing as a constraint satisfaction problem. A grammar is defined as a set of constraints on well-formed dependency graphs, and the parsing problem amounts to finding a dependency graph for a sentence that satisfies all the constraints of the grammar. Some approaches allow soft, weighted constraints and score dependency graphs by a combination of the weights of constraints violated by that graph. Parsing then becomes the problem of finding the dependency graph for a sentence that has the best score, which is essentially the same formulation as in graph-based parsing.

We can sum up our coverage of dependency parsing methods as follows:

- Data-driven dependency parsing

    - Transition-based dependency parsing (chapter 3)

    - Graph-based dependency parsing (chapter 4)

- Grammar-based parsing (chapter 5)

    - Context-free dependency parsing

    - Constraint-based dependency parsing

In chapter 6, we discuss issues concerning evaluation, both the evaluation of dependency parsers and the use of dependencies as a basis for cross-framework evaluation, and in chapter 7, we compare the approaches treated in earlier chapters, pointing out similarities and differences between methods, as well as complementary strengths and weaknesses. We conclude the book with some reflections on current trends and future prospects of dependency parsing in chapter 8.

1.3 SUMMARY AND FURTHER READING

In this chapter, we have introduced the basic notions of dependency grammar, compared dependency structure to phrase structure, and discussed criteria for identifying dependency relations and syntactic heads. There are several textbooks that give a general introduction to dependency grammar but most of them in other languages than English, for example, Tarvainen (1982) and Weber (1997) in German and Nikula (1986) in Swedish. For a basic introduction in English we refer to the opening chapter of Mel'čuk (1988). Open issues in dependency grammar, and their treatment in different theories, are discussed in chapter 3 of Nivre (2006b).

Tesnière's seminal work was published posthumously as Tesnière (1959). (The French text has been translated into German and Russian but not into English.) Other influential theories in the dependency grammar tradition include Functional Generative Description (Sgall et al., 1986); Meaning-Text Theory (Mel'čuk, 1988; Milicevic, 2006); Word Grammar (Hudson, 1984, 1990, 2007); Dependency Unification Grammar (Hellwig, 1986, 2003); and Lexicase (Starosta, 1988). Constraint-based theories of dependency grammar have a strong tradition, represented by Constraint Dependency Grammar, originally proposed by Maruyama (1990) and further developed by Harper and Helzerman (1995) and Menzel and Schröder (1998) into Weighted Constraint Dependency Grammar (Schröder, 2002); Functional Dependency Grammar (Tapanainen and Järvinen, 1997; Järvinen and Tapanainen, 1998), largely developed from Constraint Grammar (Karlsson, 1990; Karlsson et al., 1995); and finally Topological Dependency Grammar (Duchier and Debusmann, 2001), later evolved into Extensible Dependency Grammar (Debusmann et al., 2004).

In the second half of the chapter, we have given an informal introduction to dependency parsing and presented an overview of the most important approaches in this field, both data-driven and grammar-based. A more thorough discussion of different approaches can be found in chapter 3 of Nivre (2006b). Grammar-based dependency parsing originates with the work on context-free dependency parsing by Gaifman and Hays in the 1960s (Hays, 1964; Gaifman, 1965), and the constraint-based approach was first proposed by Maruyama (1990). Data-driven dependency parsing was pioneered by Eisner (1996b), using graph-based methods, and the transition-based approach was first explored by Matsumoto and colleagues (Kudo and Matsumoto, 2002; Yamada and Matsumoto, 2003). The terms *graph-based* and *transition-based* to characterize the two classes of data-driven methods were first used by McDonald and Nivre (2007), but essentially the same distinction was proposed earlier by Buchholz and Marsi (2006), using the terms *all pairs* and *stepwise*.

Although we concentrate in this book on supervised methods for data-driven parsing, there is also a considerable body of work on *unsupervised* parsing, which does not require annotated training data, although the results are so far vastly inferior to supervised approaches in terms of parsing accuracy. The interested reader is referred to Yuret (1998), Klein (2005), and Smith (2006).

Dependency parsing has recently been used in a number of different applications of natural language processing. Relevant examples include language modeling (Chelba et al., 1997), information extraction (Culotta and Sorensen, 2004), machine translation (Ding and Palmer, 2004; Quirk et al.,

2005), textual entailment (Haghighi et al., 2005), lexical ontology induction (Snow et al., 2005), and question answering (Wang et al., 2007).

CHAPTER 2

Dependency Parsing

In this chapter we formally introduce dependency graphs and dependency parsing, as well as the primary notation used throughout the rest of the book.

2.1 DEPENDENCY GRAPHS AND TREES

As mentioned in the previous chapter, dependency graphs are syntactic structures over sentences.

Definition 2.1. A *sentence* is a sequence of tokens denoted by:

$$S = w_0 w_1 \ldots w_n$$

We assume that the tokenization of a sentence is fixed and known at parsing time. That is to say that dependency parsers will always operate on a pre-tokenized input and are not responsible for producing the correct tokenization of an arbitrary string. Furthermore, $w_0 = \text{ROOT}$ is an artificial root token inserted at the beginning of the sentence and does not modify any other token in the sentence. Each token w_i typically represents a word and we will use *word* and *token* interchangeably. However, the precise definition of w_i is often language dependent and a token can be a morpheme or a punctuation marker. In particular, it is not uncommon in highly inflected languages to tokenize a sentence aggressively so that w_i can be either a lemma or the affix of a word.

For simplicity we assume that a sentence is a sequence of *unique* tokens/words. Consider the sentence:

Mary saw John and Fred saw Susan.

This sentence contains two different instances of the word *saw* and we assume each to be distinct from the other. It is straight-forward to ensure this by simply storing an index referencing the position of every word in the sequence. We assume such indices exist, even though we do not explicitly mark their presence.

Definition 2.2. Let $R = \{r_1, \ldots, r_m\}$ be a finite set of possible *dependency relation types* that can hold between any two words in a sentence. A relation type $r \in R$ is additionally called an *arc label*.

For example, the dependency relation between the words *had* and *effect* in figure 1.1 is labeled with the type $r = \text{OBJ}$. As stated earlier, we make no specific assumptions about the nature of R except that it contains a fixed inventory of dependency types.

With these two definitions in hand, we can now define dependency graphs.

Definition 2.3.   A *dependency graph* $G = (V, A)$ is a labeled directed graph (digraph) in the standard graph-theoretic sense and consists of nodes, V, and arcs, A, such that for sentence $S = w_0 w_1 \ldots w_n$ and label set R the following holds:

1. $V \subseteq \{w_0, w_1, \ldots, w_n\}$

2. $A \subseteq V \times R \times V$

3. if $(w_i, r, w_j) \in A$ then $(w_i, r', w_j) \notin A$ for all $r' \neq r$

The arc set A represents the labeled dependency relations of the particular analysis G. Specifically, an arc $(w_i, r, w_j) \in A$ represents a dependency relation from head w_i to dependent w_j labeled with relation type r. A dependency graph G is thus a set of labeled dependency relations between the words of S.

Nodes in the graph correspond directly to words in the sentence and we will use the terms node and word interchangeably. A standard node set is the *spanning node set* that contains all the words of the sentence, which we sometimes denote by $V_S = \{w_0, w_1, \ldots, w_n\}$.

Without the third restriction, dependency graphs would be *multi-digraphs* as they would allow more than one possible arc between each pair of nodes, i.e., one arc per label in R. This definition of dependency graphs is specific to mono-stratal theories of syntactic dependencies, where the entire dependency analysis is relative to a single graph over the words of the sentence. In contrast, multi-stratal theories like Functional Generative Description, Meaning-Text Theory or Topological Dependency Grammar assume that the true dependency analysis consists of multiple dependency graphs, each typically representing one layer of the analysis such as the morphological, syntactic, or semantic dependency analysis.

To illustrate this definition, consider the dependency graph in figure 1.1, which is represented by:

1. $G = (V, A)$

2. $V = V_S = \{\text{ROOT, Economic, news, had, little, effect, on, financial, markets, .}\}$

3. $A = \{(\text{ROOT, PRED, had}), (\text{had, SBJ, news}), (\text{had, OBJ, effect}), (\text{had, PU, .}),$
   $(\text{news, ATT, Economic}), (\text{effect, ATT, little}), (\text{effect, ATT, on}), (\text{on, PC, markets}),$
   $(\text{markets, ATT, financial})\}$

As discussed in the first chapter, the nature of a dependency (w_i, r, w_j) is not always straight-forward to define and differs across linguistic theories. For the remainder of this book we assume that it is fixed, being either specified by a formal grammar or implicit in a labeled corpus of dependency graphs.

Finally, having defined sentences, dependency relation types and dependency graphs, we can now proceed to a central definition,

Definition 2.4.   A *well-formed dependency graph* $G = (V, A)$ for an input sentence S and dependency relation set R is any dependency graph that is a *directed tree originating out of node* w_0 and has the spanning node set $V = V_S$. We call such dependency graphs *dependency trees*.

Notation 2.5.   For an input sentence S and a dependency relation set R, denote the space of all well-formed dependency graphs as $\mathcal{G}_S$.

The dependency graphs in figures 1.1 and 1.3 are both trees. For the remainder of the book we only consider parsing systems that produce dependency trees, that is, parsing systems that produce a tree from the set $\mathcal{G}_S$ for a sentence S.

The restriction of well-formed dependency graphs to dependency trees may seem rather strong at first given the flexibility of language. However, most mono-stratal dependency theories make this assumption (a notable exception being Hudson's Word Grammar) as do most multi-stratal theories for each individual layer of the analysis. In the next section we break down the various properties of dependency trees and examine each from a linguistic or computational point of view. Many of these properties are generally agreed upon across different dependency theories and will help to motivate the restriction of well-formed dependency graphs to trees.

2.1.1   PROPERTIES OF DEPENDENCY TREES
First, we will define a few notational conventions that will assist in our analysis of dependency trees.

Notation 2.6.   The notation $w_i \rightarrow w_j$ indicates the *unlabeled dependency relation* (or *dependency relation* for short) in a tree $G = (V, A)$. That is, $w_i \rightarrow w_j$ if and only if $(w_i, r, w_j) \in A$ for some $r \in R$.

Notation 2.7.   The notation $w_i \rightarrow^* w_j$ indicates the *reflexive transitive closure of the dependency relation* in a tree $G = (V, A)$. That is, $w_i \rightarrow^* w_j$ if and only if $i = j$ (reflexive) or both $w_i \rightarrow^* w_{i'}$ and $w_{i'} \rightarrow w_j$ hold (for some $w_{i'} \in V$).

Notation 2.8.   The notation $w_i \leftrightarrow w_j$ indicates the *undirected dependency relation* in a tree $G = (V, A)$. That is, $w_i \leftrightarrow w_j$ if and only if either $w_i \rightarrow w_j$ or $w_j \rightarrow w_i$.

Notation 2.9.   The notation $w_i \leftrightarrow^* w_j$ indicates the *reflexive transitive closure of the undirected dependency relation* in a tree $G = (V, A)$. That is, $w_i \leftrightarrow^* w_j$ if and only if $i = j$ (reflexive) or both $w_i \leftrightarrow^* w_{i'}$ and $w_{i'} \leftrightarrow w_j$ hold (for some $w_{i'} \in V$).

With this notation in hand, we can now examine a set of dependency tree properties that are always true. These properties are true of any directed tree, but we examine them from the perspective of their linguistic motivation.

Property 2.10.   A dependency tree $G = (V, A)$ always satisfies the *root property*, which states that there does not exist $w_i \in V$ such that $w_i \to w_0$.

Property 2.10 holds from the definition of dependency trees as rooted directed trees originating out of w_0. This property is artificial since we have already indicated the presence of the word ROOT and defined its unique nature in the definition of dependency trees. The addition of an artificial root node may seem spurious, but as we discuss subsequent properties below, it will become clear that the artificial root provides us with both linguistic and algorithmic generalization ability.

Property 2.11.   A dependency tree $G = (V, A)$ always satisfies the *spanning property* over the words of the sentence, which states that $V = V_S$.

Property 2.11 is also explicitly stated in the definition of dependency trees and therefore must hold for all dependency trees. The spanning property is widely accepted in dependency theories since a word in a sentence almost always has some relevance to the dependency analysis and in particular the syntactic analysis of the sentence. This property is sometimes relaxed for punctuation, for example words like periods or other sentence boundary markers that play no role in the dependency analysis of the sentence. The property may be further relaxed for additional punctuation such as hyphens and brackets – as well as some comma usage – that implicitly participate in the analysis by providing cues for the intended reading but again play no explicit role in the analysis. When considering semantic dependencies the spanning property is less universal as many words simply facilitate the reader's understanding of the true semantic interpretation and do not actually have an explicit semantic function.

　　In practice it is irrelevant if linguistic theories agree on whether a dependency analysis should be spanning over all the words in the sentence. This is because the artificial root node allows one to be theory general with respect to the spanning property as we can simply create an arc from the root word to all $w_i \in V$ that do not participate in the analysis. The result is always a dependency tree where the spanning property holds.

Property 2.12.   A dependency tree $G = (V, A)$ satisfies the *connectedness property*, which states that for all $w_i, w_j \in V$ it is the case that $w_i \leftrightarrow^* w_j$. That is, there is a path connecting every two words in a dependency tree when the direction of the arc (dependency relation) is ignored. This notion of connectedness is equivalent to a *weakly connected directed graph* from graph theory.

Property 2.12 holds due to the fact that all nodes in a directed tree are weakly connected through the root. The connectedness property simply states that all words in the sentence interact with one another in the dependency analysis, even if at a distance or through intermediate words. This property is not universally accepted, as a sentence may be fragmented into a number of disjoint units. However, we can again use the artificial root word and make this property universal by simply creating a dependency relation from the root to some word in each of the dependency fragments. Thus, the artificial root word again allows one to be theory-neutral, this time with respect to dependency analysis connectedness. Furthermore, we also gain a computational generalization through the artificial root node. As we will see in Chapter 3, some dependency parsing algorithms do not actually produce a single dependency tree but rather a set of disjoint dependency trees, commonly called a *dependency forest*. These algorithms can be trivially modified to return a dependency tree by adding a dependency arc from the artificial root word to the root of each disjoint tree.

Property 2.13.   A dependency tree $G = (V, A)$ satisfies the *single-head property*, which states that for all $w_i, w_j \in V$, if $w_i \to w_j$ then there does not exist $w_{i'} \in V$ such that $i' \neq i$ and $w_{i'} \to w_j$. That is, each word in a dependency tree is the dependent of at most one head.

Property 2.13 holds due to the fact that a directed tree is specifically characterized by each node having a single incoming arc. The single-head property is not universal in dependency theories. The example from chapter 1 – *She bought and ate an apple* – is an instance where one might wish to break the single-head property. In particular, *she* and *apple* can be viewed as dependents of both verbs in the coordinated verb phrase and as a result should participate as the dependent in multiple dependency arcs in the tree. However, many formalisms simply posit that *she* and *apple* modify the head of the coordinate phrase (whether it is the conjunction or one of the verbs) and assume that this dependency is propagated to all the conjuncts.

Property 2.14.   A dependency tree $G = (V, A)$ satisfies the *acyclicity property*, which states that for all $w_i, w_j \in A$, if $w_i \to w_j$, then it is not the case that $w_j \to^* w_i$. That is, a dependency tree does not contains cycles.

The acyclicity property also makes sense linguistically as any dependency tree not satisfying this property would imply that a word implicitly is dependent upon itself.

Property 2.15.   A dependency tree $G = (V, A)$ satisfies the *arc size property*, which states that $|A| = |V| - 1$.

Property 2.15 falls out of the unique root and single-head properties. We listed this property as it can simplify both algorithm construction and analysis.

2.1.2   PROJECTIVE DEPENDENCY TREES

Up to this point we have presented properties that hold for all dependency trees. However, many computational systems restrict the class of well-formed dependency graphs even further. The most common restriction is to the set of *projective dependency trees*, which we examine here.

Definition 2.16.   An arc $(w_i, r, w_j) \in A$ in a dependency tree $G = (V, A)$ is *projective* if and only if $w_i \to^* w_k$ for all $i < k < j$ when $i < j$, or $j < k < i$ when $j < i$.

That is to say, an arc in a tree is projective if there is a directed path from the head word w_i to all the words between the two endpoints of the arc.

Definition 2.17.   A dependency tree $G = (V, A)$ is a *projective dependency tree* if (1) it is a dependency tree (definition 2.4), and (2) all $(w_i, r, w_j) \in A$ are projective.

A similar definition exists for *non-projective dependency trees*.

Definition 2.18.   A dependency tree $G = (V, A)$ is a *non-projective dependency tree* if (1) it is a dependency tree (definition 2.4), and (2) it is not projective.

The trees in figures 1.1 and 1.3 are both projective dependency trees. Linguistically, projectivity is too rigid a restriction. Consider the sentence in figure 2.1. The dependency tree for this sentence is *non-projective* since the prepositional phrase *on the issue* that modifies the noun *hearing* is separated sequentially from its head by the main verb group. As a result, the dependency (hearing, PP, on) does not satisfy the projective arc definition, requiring a non-projective analysis to account for the syntactic validity of this sentence.

In English, non-projective constructions occur with little frequency relative to other languages that are highly inflected and, as a result, have less constraints on word order. In particular, sentences in languages like Czech, Dutch and Turkish frequently require non-projective dependency trees to correctly analyze a significant fraction of sentences. As a result, most linguistic theories of dependency parsing do not presume that dependency trees are projective. Thus, throughout most of this book we will not assume that dependency trees are projective and make it clear when we are referring to the set of all dependency trees, or the subset of projective dependency trees.

Notation 2.19.   For an input sentence S and a dependency relation set R, denote the space of all projective dependency trees as $\mathcal{G}_S^p$.

Even though they are too restrictive, projective dependency trees have certain properties of interest, primarily from a computational perspective.

Property 2.20.   A projective dependency tree $G = (V, A)$ satisfies the *planar property*, which states that it is possible to graphically configure all the arcs of the tree in the space above the sentence without any arcs crossing.

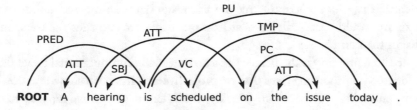

Figure 2.1: Non-projective dependency tree for an English sentence.

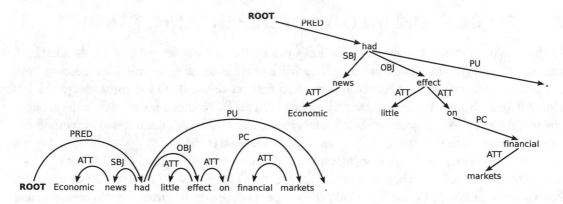

Figure 2.2: Projective dependency tree drawn in the standard way (left) and as a nested tree (right).

The left tree in figure 2.2 displays a projective tree drawn without arc crossings, whereas the tree in figure 2.1 shows a non-projective tree where it is impossible to configure the arcs so that none cross. The inverse of this property is true as well: all dependency trees that can be drawn so that no arcs cross are projective dependency trees. This direction of the equivalence specifically relies on the fact that the left-most word in the sentence is the root of the tree. Consider the case where $S = w_0 w_1 w_2$ with arcs $w_0 \rightarrow w_2$ and $w_1 \rightarrow w_0$ in a dependency tree G, i.e., w_1 is the root. Such a tree can be drawn with no arcs crossing, but is not projective.

Property 2.21. A projective dependency tree $G = (V, A)$ satisfies the *nested property*, which states that for all nodes $w_i \in V$, the set of words $\{w_j | w_i \rightarrow^* w_j\}$ is a contiguous subsequence of the sentence S.

The set $\{w_j | w_i \rightarrow^* w_j\}$ is often called the *yield* of w_i in G. Figure 2.2 illustrates both a projective dependency tree and its nested depiction. Proving that all projective dependency trees are nested trees is straight-forward. If we assume that the yield of w_i is not contiguous, that means that there is some node w_j between the end-points of the yield such that $w_i \rightarrow^* w_j$ does not hold. If we trace dependency arcs back from w_j we will eventually reach a node w_k between the end-points of the yield of w_i such that $w_{k'} \rightarrow w_k$ is in the tree but $w_{k'}$ is not between the end-points of the yield of w_i. But such an arc would necessarily cross at least one other arc and thus the tree could not have been projective in the first place.

The nested tree property is the primary reason that many computational dependency parsing systems have focused on producing trees that are projective as it has been shown that certain dependency grammars enforcing projectivity are (weakly) equivalent in generative capacity to context-free grammars, which are well understood computationally from both complexity and formal power standpoints.

2.2   FORMAL DEFINITION OF DEPENDENCY PARSING

In this section, we aim to make mathematically precise the dependency parsing problem for both data-driven and grammar-based methods. This will include introducing notation and defining both the general problems of *learning*, which is required for data-driven methods, and *parsing*, which is required for both data-driven and grammar-based methods. To reiterate a point made in the previous chapter, data-driven and grammar-based methods are compatible. A grammar-based method can be data-driven when its parameters are learned from a labeled corpus.

As with our earlier convention, we use G to indicate a dependency tree and $\mathcal{G}$ to indicate a set of dependency trees. Similarly, $S = w_0 w_1 \ldots w_n$ denotes a sentence and $\mathcal{S}$ denotes a set of sentences. For a given sentence S, we use $\mathcal{G}_S$ to indicate the space of dependency trees for that sentence, and we use $\mathcal{G}_S^p$ for the subset of projective dependency trees.

An important function that will be used at various points throughout the book is the feature function $\mathbf{f}(x) : \mathcal{X} \rightarrow \mathcal{Y}$ that maps some input x to a feature representation in the space $\mathcal{Y}$. Examples include mappings from an input sentence S or history of parsing decisions to a set of predictive symbolic or binary predicates. When $\mathcal{Y}$ is a collection of predicates (either symbolic or numeric), then we often refer to $\mathbf{f}$ as the *feature vector*. Possibly the most common mapping for $\mathbf{f}$ is to a high dimensional real valued feature vector, i.e., $\mathcal{Y} = \mathbb{R}^m$. The features used in a parsing system differ by the parsing scheme and will be discussed in further detail in later chapters.

Let us now proceed with an important definition:

Definition 2.22.   A *dependency parsing model* consists of a set of constraints Γ that define the space of permissible dependency structures for a given sentence, a set of parameters $\boldsymbol{\lambda}$ (possibly null), and fixed parsing algorithm h. A model is denoted by $M = (\Gamma, \boldsymbol{\lambda}, h)$.

The constraints Γ are specific to the underlying formalism used by a system. Minimally the constraint set maps an arbitrary sentence S and dependency type set R to the set of well-formed dependency graphs $\mathcal{G}_S$, in effect restricting the space of dependency graphs to dependency trees. Additionally, Γ could encode more complex mechanisms such as context-free grammar or a constraint dependency grammar that further limit the space of dependency graphs.

The *learning* phase of a parser aims to construct the parameter set λ, and it is specific to data-driven systems. The parameters are learned using a training set $\mathcal{D}$ that consists of pairs of sentences and their corresponding dependency trees:

$$\mathcal{D} = \{(S_d, G_d)\}_{d=0}^{|\mathcal{D}|}$$

Parameters are typically learned by optimizing some function over $\mathcal{D}$ and come from some predefined class of parameters Λ. Common optimizations include minimizing training set parsing error or maximizing conditional probability of trees given sentences for examples in $\mathcal{D}$. The nature of λ and the optimization depend on the specific learning methods employed. For example, a single parameter might represent the likelihood of a dependency arc occurring in a dependency tree for a sentence, or it might represent the likelihood of satisfying some preference in a formal grammar. In the following chapters, these specifics will be addressed when we examine the major approaches to dependency parsing. For systems that are not data-driven, λ is either null or uniform rendering it irrelevant.

After a parsing model has defined a set of formal constraints and learned appropriate parameters, the model must fix a parsing algorithm to solve the *parsing* problem. That is, given the constraints, parameters and a new sentence S, how does the system find the single most likely dependency tree for that sentence:

$$G = h(S, \Gamma, \lambda)$$

The function h is a search over the set of well-formed dependency graphs $\mathcal{G}_S$ for input sentence S and produces a single tree or null if Γ defines a grammar in which S is not a member of the defined language. As we will see in the remaining chapters, h can take many algorithmic forms including greedy and recursive algorithms as well as those based on chart-parsing techniques. Furthermore, h can be exact or approximate relative to some objective function.

To give a quick illustration of the notation defined here, we can apply it to the well known case of a probabilistic context-free grammar (PCFG) for phrase structure parsing – a grammar-based and data-driven parsing system. In that case, $\Gamma = (N, \Sigma, \Pi, \text{START})$ is a standard CFG with non-terminals N, terminals Σ, production rules Π, and start symbol $\text{START} \in N$, all of which defines a space of nested phrase structures. λ is a set of probabilities, one for each production in the grammar. λ is typically set by maximizing the likelihood of the training set $\mathcal{D}$ relative to appropriate consistency constraints. The fixed parsing algorithm h can then be a number of context-free algorithms such as CKY (Younger, 1967) or Earley's algorithm (Earley, 1970).

2.3   SUMMARY AND FURTHER READING

In this chapter, we discussed the formal definition of dependency graphs, as well as a set of properties of these graphs that are common among many systems (both linguistic and computational). A key definition is that of a dependency tree, which is any well-formed dependency graph that is a directed spanning tree originating out of the root word w_0. There have been many studies of the structural properties of dependency graphs and trees that go beyond what is discussed here. Mentioned earlier was work showing that certain projective dependency grammars are weakly equivalent to context-free grammars (Hays, 1964; Gaifman, 1965). Structural properties of dependency graphs that have been studied include: *planarity*, which is strongly correlated to projectivity (Kuhlmann and Nivre, 2006; Havelka, 2007); *gap-degree*, which measures the discontinuity of subgraphs (Bodirsky et al., 2005; Kuhlmann and Nivre, 2006); *well-nestedness*, which is a binary property on the overlap between subtrees of the graph (Bodirsky et al., 2005; Kuhlmann and Nivre, 2006); and *arc-degree*, which measures the number of disconnected subgraphs an arc spans in the graph (Nivre, 2006a; Kuhlmann and Nivre, 2006). Some interesting facts arise out of these studies. This includes the relation of dependency graph structural constraints to derivations in tree adjoining grammars (Bodirsky et al., 2005) as well as empirical statistics on how frequently certain constraints are obeyed in various dependency treebanks (Nivre, 2006a; Kuhlmann and Nivre, 2006; Havelka, 2007). In terms of projectivity, Marcus (1965) proves the equivalence of a variety of projectivity definitions and Havelka (2007) discusses many of the above properties in relation to the projective constraint.

The final section of this chapter introduced the formal definition of dependency parsing including the definition of a parsing model and its sub-components: the formal constraints, the parameters, and the parsing algorithm. These definitions, as well as those given for dependency trees, form the basis for the next chapters that delve into different parsing formalisms and their relation to one another.

CHAPTER 3

Transition-Based Parsing

In data-driven dependency parsing, the goal is to learn a good predictor of dependency trees, that is, a model that can be used to map an input sentence $S = w_0 w_1 \ldots w_n$ to its correct dependency tree G. As explained in the previous chapter, such a model has the general form $M = (\Gamma, \lambda, h)$, where Γ is a set of constraints that define the space of permissible structures for a given sentence, λ is a set of parameters, the values of which have to be learned from data, and h is a fixed parsing algorithm. In this chapter, we are going to look at systems that parameterize a model over the transitions of an abstract machine for deriving dependency trees, where we learn to predict the next transition given the input and the parse history, and where we predict new trees using a greedy, deterministic parsing algorithm – this is what we call transition-based parsing. In chapter 4, we will instead consider systems that parameterize a model over sub-structures of dependency trees, where we learn to score entire dependency trees given the input, and where we predict new trees using exact inference – graph-based parsing. Since most transition-based and graph-based systems do not make use of a formal grammar at all, Γ will typically only restrict the possible dependency trees for a sentence to those that satisfy certain formal constraints, for example, the set of all projective trees (over a given label set). In chapter 5, by contrast, we will deal with grammar-based systems, where Γ constitutes a formal grammar pairing each input sentence with a more restricted (possibly empty) set of dependency trees.

3.1 TRANSITION SYSTEMS

A *transition system* is an abstract machine, consisting of a set of *configurations* (or *states*) and *transitions* between configurations. One of the simplest examples is a finite state automaton, which consists of a finite set of atomic states and transitions defined on states and input symbols, and which accepts an input string if there is a sequence of valid transitions from a designated *initial* state to one of several *terminal* states. By contrast, the transition systems used for dependency parsing have complex configurations with internal structure, instead of atomic states, and transitions that correspond to steps in the derivation of a dependency tree. The idea is that a sequence of valid transitions, starting in the initial configuration for a given sentence and ending in one of several terminal configurations, defines a valid dependency tree for the input sentence. In this way, the transition system determines the constraint set Γ in the parsing model, since it implicitly defines the set of permissible dependency trees for a given sentence, but it also determines the parameter set λ that have to be learned from data, as we shall see later on. For most of this chapter, we will concentrate on a simple stack-based transition system, which implements a form of shift-reduce parsing and exemplifies the most widely used approach in transition-based dependency parsing. In section 3.4, we will briefly discuss some of the alternative systems that have been proposed.

We start by defining configurations as triples consisting of a stack, an input buffer, and a set of dependency arcs.

Definition 3.1. Given a set R of dependency types, a *configuration* for a sentence $S = w_0 w_1 \ldots w_n$ is a triple $c = (\sigma, \beta, A)$, where

1. σ is a stack of words $w_i \in V_S$,

2. β is a buffer of words $w_i \in V_S$,

3. A is a set of dependency arcs $(w_i, r, w_j) \in V_S \times R \times V_S$.

The idea is that a configuration represents a partial analysis of the input sentence, where the words on the stack σ are partially processed words, the words in the buffer β are the remaining input words, and the arc set A represents a partially built dependency tree. For example, if the input sentence is

Economic news had little effect on financial markets.

then the following is a valid configuration, where the stack contains the words ROOT and *news* (with the latter on top), the buffer contains all the remaining words except *Economic*, and the arc set contains a single arc connecting the head *news* to the dependent *Economic* with the label ATT:

([ROOT, news]$_\sigma$, [had, little, effect, on, financial, markets, .]$_\beta$, {(news, ATT, Economic)}$_A$)

Note that we represent both the stack and the buffer as simple lists, with elements enclosed in square brackets (and subscripts σ and β when needed), although the stack has its head (or top) to the right for reasons of perspicuity. When convenient, we use the notation $\sigma | w_i$ to represent the stack which results from pushing w_i onto the stack σ, and we use $w_i | \beta$ to represent a buffer with head w_i and tail β.[1]

Definition 3.2. For any sentence $S = w_0 w_1 \ldots w_n$,

1. the *initial* configuration $c_0(S)$ is ([w_0]$_\sigma$, [$w_1, \ldots, w_n$]$_\beta$, $\emptyset$),

2. a *terminal* configuration is a configuration of the form $(\sigma, [\ ]_\beta, A)$ for any σ and A.

Thus, we initialize the system to a configuration with w_0 = ROOT on the stack, all the remaining words in the buffer, and an empty arc set; and we terminate in any configuration that has an empty buffer (regardless of the state of the stack and the arc set).

---

[1] The operator | is taken to be left-associative for the stack and right-associative for the buffer.

Transition		Precondition
LEFT-ARC$_r$	$(\sigma\|w_i, w_j\|\beta, A) \Rightarrow (\sigma, w_j\|\beta, A\cup\{(w_j, r, w_i)\})$	$i \neq 0$
RIGHT-ARC$_r$	$(\sigma\|w_i, w_j\|\beta, A) \Rightarrow (\sigma, w_i\|\beta, A\cup\{(w_i, r, w_j)\})$	
SHIFT	$(\sigma, w_i\|\beta, A) \Rightarrow (\sigma\|w_i, \beta, A)$	

Figure 3.1: Transitions for shift-reduce dependency parsing.

Having defined the set of configurations, including a unique initial configuration and a set of terminal configurations for any sentence, we now define transitions between configurations. Formally speaking, a transition is a partial function from configurations to configurations, i.e., a transition maps a given configuration to a new configuration but may be undefined for certain configurations. Conceptually, a transition corresponds to a basic parsing action that adds an arc to the dependency tree or modifies the stack or the buffer. The transitions needed for shift-reduce dependency parsing are defined in figure 3.1 and contain three types of transitions:

1. Transitions LEFT-ARC$_r$ (for any dependency label r) add a dependency arc (w_j, r, w_i) to the arc set A, where w_i is the word on top of the stack and w_j is the first word in the buffer. In addition, they pop the stack. They have as precondition that both the stack and the buffer are non-empty and that $w_i \neq$ ROOT.[2]

2. Transitions RIGHT-ARC$_r$ (for any dependency label r) add a dependency arc (w_i, r, w_j) to the arc set A, where w_i is the word on top of the stack and w_j is the first word in the buffer. In addition, they pop the stack and replace w_j by w_i at the head of buffer.[3] They have as their only precondition that both the stack and the buffer are non-empty.

3. The transition SHIFT removes the first word w_i in the buffer and pushes it on top of the stack. It has as its only precondition that the buffer is non-empty.

We use the symbol $\mathcal{T}$ to refer to the set of permissible transitions in a given transition system. As noted above, transitions correspond to elementary parsing actions. In order to define complete parses, we introduce the notion of a *transition sequence*.

Definition 3.3. A *transition sequence* for a sentence $S = w_0w_1 \ldots w_n$ is a sequence of configurations $C_{0,m} = (c_0, c_1, \ldots, c_m)$ such that

---

[2]The latter precondition guarantees that the dependency graph defined by the arc set always satisfies the root property.

[3]This may seem counterintuitive, given that the buffer is meant to contain words that have not yet been processed, but it is necessary in order to allow w_j to attach to a head on its left.

Transition		Configuration	
	([ROOT],	[Economic, ..., .],	$\emptyset$)
SH $\Rightarrow$	([ROOT, Economic],	[news, ..., .],	$\emptyset$)
LA$_{\text{ATT}}$ $\Rightarrow$	([ROOT],	[news, ..., .],	$A_1 = \{(\text{news, ATT, Economic})\})$
SH $\Rightarrow$	([ROOT, news],	[had, ..., .],	A_1)
LA$_{\text{SBJ}}$ $\Rightarrow$	([ROOT],	[had, ..., .],	$A_2 = A_1 \cup \{(\text{had, SBJ, news})\})$
SH $\Rightarrow$	([ROOT, had],	[little, ..., .],	A_2)
SH $\Rightarrow$	([ROOT, had, little],	[effect, ..., .],	A_2)
LA$_{\text{ATT}}$ $\Rightarrow$	([ROOT, had],	[effect, ..., .],	$A_3 = A_2 \cup \{(\text{effect, ATT, little})\})$
SH $\Rightarrow$	([ROOT, had, effect],	[on, ..., .],	A_3)
SH $\Rightarrow$	([ROOT, ... on],	[financial, markets, .],	A_3)
SH $\Rightarrow$	([ROOT, ..., financial],	[markets, .],	A_3)
LA$_{\text{ATT}}$ $\Rightarrow$	([ROOT, ... on],	[markets, .],	$A_4 = A_3 \cup \{(\text{markets, ATT, financial})\})$
RA$_{\text{PC}}$ $\Rightarrow$	([ROOT, had, effect],	[on, .],	$A_5 = A_4 \cup \{(\text{on, PC, markets})\})$
RA$_{\text{ATT}}$ $\Rightarrow$	([ROOT, had],	[effect, .],	$A_6 = A_5 \cup \{(\text{effect, ATT, on})\})$
RA$_{\text{OBJ}}$ $\Rightarrow$	([ROOT],	[had, .],	$A_7 = A_6 \cup \{(\text{had, OBJ, effect})\})$
SH $\Rightarrow$	([ROOT, had],	[.],	A_7)
RA$_{\text{PU}}$ $\Rightarrow$	([ROOT],	[had],	$A_8 = A_7 \cup \{(\text{had, PU, .})\})$
RA$_{\text{PRED}}$ $\Rightarrow$	([ ],	[ROOT],	$A_9 = A_8 \cup \{(\text{ROOT, PRED, had})\})$
SH $\Rightarrow$	([ROOT],	[ ],	A_9)

Figure 3.2: Transition sequence for the English sentence in figure 1.1 (LA$_r$ = LEFT-ARC$_r$, RA$_r$ = RIGHT-ARC$_r$, SH = SHIFT).

1. c_0 is the initial configuration $c_0(S)$ for S,

2. c_m is a terminal configuration,

3. for every i such that $1 \leq i \leq m$, there is a transition $t \in \mathcal{T}$ such that $c_i = t(c_{i-1})$.

A transition sequence starts in the initial configuration for a given sentence and reaches a terminal configuration by applying valid transitions from one configuration to the next. The dependency tree derived through this transition sequence is the dependency tree defined by the terminal configuration, i.e., the tree $G_{c_m} = (V_S, A_{c_m})$, where A_{c_m} is the arc set in the terminal configuration c_m. By way of example, figure 3.2 shows a transition sequence that derives the dependency tree shown in figure 1.1 on page 2.

The transition system defined for dependency parsing in this section leads to derivations that correspond to basic shift-reduce parsing for context-free grammars. The LEFT-ARC$_r$ and RIGHT-ARC$_r$ transitions correspond to reduce actions, replacing a head-dependent structure with its head, while the SHIFT transition is exactly the same as the shift action. One peculiarity of the transitions, as defined here, is that the "reduce transitions" apply to one node on the stack and one node in the buffer, rather than two nodes on the stack. This simplifies the definition of terminal configurations and has become standard in the dependency parsing literature.

Every transition sequence in this system defines a dependency graph with the *spanning*, *root*, and *single-head* properties, but not necessarily with the *connectedness* property. This means that not every transition sequence defines a dependency tree, as defined in chapter 2. To take a trivial example, a transition sequence for a sentence S consisting only of SHIFT transitions defines the graph $G = (V_S, \emptyset)$, which is not connected but which satisfies all the other properties. However, since any transition sequence defines an *acyclic* dependency graph G, it is trivial to convert G into a dependency tree G' by adding arcs of the form (ROOT, r, w_i) (with some dependency label r) for every w_i that is a root in G. As noted in section 2.1.1, a dependency graph G that satisfies the spanning, root, single-head, and acyclic properties is equivalent to a set of dependency trees and is often called a *dependency forest*.

Another important property of the system is that every transition sequence defines a *projective* dependency forest,[4] which is advantageous from the point of view of efficiency but overly restrictive from the point of view of representational adequacy. In sections 3.4 and 3.5, we will see how this limitation can be overcome, either by modifying the transition system or by complementing it with pre- and post-processing.

Given that every transition sequence defines a projective dependency forest, which can be turned into a dependency tree, we say that the system is *sound* with respect to the set of projective dependency trees. A natural question is whether the system is also *complete* with respect to this class of dependency trees, that is, whether every projective dependency tree is defined by some transition sequence. The answer to this question is affirmative, although we will not prove it here.[5] In terms of our parsing model $M = (\Gamma, \boldsymbol{\lambda}, h)$, we can therefore say that the transition system described in this section corresponds to a set of constraints Γ characterizing the set $\mathcal{G}_S^p$ of projective dependency trees for a given sentence S (relative to a set of arc labels R).

3.2 PARSING ALGORITHM

The transition system defined in section 3.1 is nondeterministic in the sense that there is usually more than one transition that is valid for any non-terminal configuration.[6] Thus, in order to perform deterministic parsing, we need a mechanism to determine for any non-terminal configuration c, what is the correct transition out of c. Let us assume for the time being that we are given an *oracle*, that is, a function o from configurations to transitions such that $o(c) = t$ if and only if t is the correct transition out of c. Given such an oracle, deterministic parsing can be achieved by the very simple algorithm in figure 3.3.

We start in the initial configuration $c_0(S)$ and, as long as we have not reached a terminal configuration, we use the oracle to find the optimal transition $t = o(c)$ and apply it to our current configuration to reach the next configuration $t(c)$. Once we reach a terminal configuration, we simply return the dependency tree defined by our current arc set. Note that, while finding the

---

[4]A dependency forest is projective if and only if all component trees are projective.

[5]The interested reader is referred to Nivre (2008) for proofs of soundness and completeness for this and several other transition systems for dependency parsing.

[6]The notable exception is a configuration with an empty stack, where only SHIFT is possible.

$\mathbf{h}(S, \Gamma, o)$
1    $c \leftarrow c_0(S)$
2   **while** c is not terminal
3              $t \leftarrow o(c)$
4              $c \leftarrow t(c)$
5   **return** G_c

Figure 3.3: Deterministic, transition-based parsing with an oracle.

optimal transition $t = o(c)$ is a hard problem, which we have to tackle using machine learning, computing the next configuration $t(c)$ is a purely mechanical operation.

It is easy to show that, as long as there is at least one valid transition for every non-terminal configuration, such a parser will construct exactly one transition sequence $C_{0,m}$ for a sentence S and return the dependency tree defined by the terminal configuration c_m, i.e., $G_{c_m} = (V_S, A_{c_m})$. To see that there is always at least one valid transition out of a non-terminal configuration, we only have to note that such a configuration must have a non-empty buffer (otherwise it would be terminal), which means that at least SHIFT is a valid transition.

The time complexity of the deterministic, transition-based parsing algorithm is $O(n)$, where n is the number of words in the input sentence S, provided that the oracle and transition functions can be computed in constant time. This holds since the worst-case running time is bounded by the maximum number of transitions in a transition sequence $C_{0,m}$ for a sentence $S = w_0 w_1 \ldots w_n$. Since a SHIFT transition decreases the length of the buffer by 1, no other transition increases the length of the buffer, and any configuration with an empty buffer is terminal, the number of SHIFT transitions in $C_{0,m}$ is bounded by n. Moreover, since both LEFT-ARC$_r$ and RIGHT-ARC$_r$ decrease the height of the stack by 1, only SHIFT increases the height of the stack by 1, and the initial height of the stack is 1, the combined number of instances of LEFT-ARC$_r$ and RIGHT-ARC$_r$ in $C_{0,m}$ is also bounded by n. Hence, the worst-case time complexity is $O(n)$.

So far, we have seen how transition-based parsing can be performed in linear time if restricted to projective dependency trees, and provided that we have a constant-time oracle that predicts the correct transition out of any non-terminal configuration. Of course, oracles are hard to come by in real life, so in order to build practical parsing systems, we need to find some other mechanism that we can use to approximate the oracle well enough to make accurate parsing feasible. There are many conceivable ways of approximating oracles, including the use of formal grammars and disambiguation heuristics. However, the most successful strategy to date has been to take a data-driven approach, approximating oracles by *classifiers* trained on treebank data. This leads to the notion of classifier-based parsing, which is an essential component of transition-based dependency parsing.

h(S, Γ, λ)
1    $c \leftarrow c_0(S)$
2   **while** c is not terminal
3        $t \leftarrow \lambda_c$
4        $c \leftarrow t(c)$
5   **return** G_c

Figure 3.4: Deterministic, transition-based parsing with a classifier.

3.3   CLASSIFIER-BASED PARSING

Let us step back for a moment to our general characterization of a data-driven parsing model as $M = (\Gamma, \lambda, h)$, where Γ is a set of constraints on dependency graphs, λ is a set of model parameters and h is a fixed parsing algorithm. In the previous two sections, we have shown how we can define the parsing algorithm h as deterministic best-first search in a transition system (although other search strategies are possible, as we shall see later on). The transition system determines the set of constraints Γ, but it also defines the model parameters λ that need to be learned from data, since we need to be able to predict the oracle transition $o(c)$ for every possible configuration c (for any input sentence S). We use the notation $\lambda_c \in \lambda$ to denote the transition predicted for c according to model parameters λ, and we can think of λ as a huge table containing the predicted transition λ_c for every possible configuration c. In practice, λ is normally a compact representation of a function for computing λ_c given c, but the details of this representation need not concern us now. Given a learned model, we can perform deterministic, transition-based parsing using the algorithm in figure 3.4, where we have simply replaced the oracle function o by the learned parameters λ (and the function value $o(c)$ by the specific parameter value λ_c).

However, in order to make the learning problem tractable by standard machine learning techniques, we need to introduce an abstraction over the infinite set of possible configurations. This is what is achieved by the feature function $\mathbf{f}(x) : \mathcal{X} \rightarrow \mathcal{Y}$ (cf. section 2.2). In our case, the domain $\mathcal{X}$ is the set $\mathcal{C}$ of possible configurations (for any sentence S) and the range $\mathcal{Y}$ is a product of m feature value sets, which means that the feature function $\mathbf{f}(c) : \mathcal{C} \rightarrow \mathcal{Y}$ maps every configuration to an m-dimensional feature vector. Given this representation, we then want to learn a classifier $g : \mathcal{Y} \rightarrow \mathcal{T}$, where $\mathcal{T}$ is the set of possible transitions, such that $g(\mathbf{f}(c)) = o(c)$ for any configuration c. In other words, given a training set of gold standard dependency trees from a treebank, we want to learn a classifier that predicts the oracle transition $o(c)$ for any configuration c, given as input the feature representation $\mathbf{f}(c)$. This gives rise to three basic questions:

- How do we represent configurations by feature vectors?

- How do we derive training data from treebanks?

- How do we train classifiers?

We will deal with each of these questions in turn, starting with feature representations in section 3.3.1, continuing with the derivation of training data in section 3.3.2, and finishing off with the training of classifiers in section 3.3.3.

3.3.1   FEATURE REPRESENTATIONS

A feature representation $\mathbf{f}(c)$ of a configuration c is an m-dimensional vector of simple features $\mathbf{f}_i(c)$ (for $1 \leq i \leq m$). In the general case, these simple features can be defined by arbitrary attributes of a configuration, which may be either categorical or numerical. For example, "the part of speech of the word on top of the stack" is a categorical feature, with values taken from a particular part-of-speech tagset (e.g., NN for noun, VB for verb, etc.). By contrast, "the number of dependents previously attached to the word on top of the stack" is a numerical feature, with values taken from the set $\{0, 1, 2, \ldots\}$. The choice of feature representations is partly dependent on the choice of learning algorithm, since some algorithms impose special restrictions on the form that feature values may take, for example, that all features must be numerical. However, in the interest of generality, we will ignore this complication for the time being and assume that features can be of either type. This is unproblematic since it is always possible to convert categorical features to numerical features, and it will greatly simplify the discussion of feature representations for transition-based parsing.

The most important features in transition-based parsing are defined by attributes of words, or tree nodes, identified by their position in the configuration. It is often convenient to think of these features as defined by two simpler functions, an *address function* identifying a particular word in a configuration (e.g., the word on top of the stack) and an *attribute function* selecting a specific attribute of this word (e.g., its part of speech). We call these features *configurational word features* and define them as follows.

Definition 3.4.   Given an input sentence $S = w_0 w_1 \ldots w_n$ with node set V_S, a function $(v \circ a)(c) : \mathcal{C} \to Y$ composed of

1. an address function $a(c) : \mathcal{C} \to V_S$,

2. an attribute function $v(w) : V_S \to Y$.

is a *configurational word feature*.

An address function can in turn be composed of simpler functions, which operate on different components of the input configuration c. For example:

- Functions that extract the kth word (from the top) of the stack or the kth word (from the head) of the buffer.

- Functions that map a word w to its parent, leftmost child, rightmost child, leftmost sibling, or rightmost sibling in the dependency graph defined by c.

Table 3.1: Feature model for transition-based parsing.

f_i	Address	Attribute
1	STK[0]	FORM
2	BUF[0]	FORM
3	BUF[1]	FORM
4	LDEP(STK[0])	DEPREL
5	RDEP(STK[0])	DEPREL
6	LDEP(BUF[0])	DEPREL
7	RDEP(BUF[0])	DEPREL

By defining such functions, we can construct arbitrarily complex address functions that extract, e.g., "the rightmost sibling of the leftmost child of the parent of the word on top of the stack" although the address functions used in practice typically combine at most three such functions. It is worth noting that most address functions are partial, which means that they may fail to return a word. For example, a function that is supposed to return the leftmost child of the word on top of the stack is undefined if the stack is empty or if the word on top of the stack does not have any children. In this case, any feature defined with this address function will also be undefined (or have a special null value).

The typical attribute functions refer to some linguistic property of words, which may be given as input to the parser or computed as part of the parsing process. We can exemplify this with the word *markets* from the sentence in figure 1.1:

- Identity of w_i = *markets*

- Identity of lemma of w_i = *market*

- Identity of part-of-speech tag for w_i = NNS

- Identity of dependency label for w_i = PC

The first three attributes are *static* in the sense that they are constant, if available at all, in every configuration for a given sentence. That is, if the input sentence has been lemmatized and tagged for parts of speech in preprocessing, then the values of these features are available for all words of the sentence, and their values do not change during parsing. By contrast, the dependency label attribute is *dynamic* in the sense that it is available only after the relevant dependency arc has been added to the arc set. Thus, in the transition sequence in figure 3.2, the dependency label for the word *markets* is undefined in the first twelve configurations, but has the value PC in all the remaining configurations. Hence, such attributes can be used to define features of the transition history and the partially built dependency tree, which turns out to be one of the major advantages of the transition-based approach.

$\mathbf{f}(c_0)$	=	(ROOT	Economic	news	NULL	NULL	NULL	NULL)
$\mathbf{f}(c_1)$	=	(Economic	news	had	NULL	NULL	NULL	NULL)
$\mathbf{f}(c_2)$	=	(ROOT	news	had	NULL	NULL	ATT	NULL)
$\mathbf{f}(c_3)$	=	(news	had	little	ATT	NULL	NULL	NULL)
$\mathbf{f}(c_4)$	=	(ROOT	had	little	NULL	NULL	SBJ	NULL)
$\mathbf{f}(c_5)$	=	(had	little	effect	SBJ	NULL	NULL	NULL)
$\mathbf{f}(c_6)$	=	(little	effect	on	NULL	NULL	NULL	NULL)
$\mathbf{f}(c_7)$	=	(had	effect	on	SBJ	NULL	ATT	NULL)
$\mathbf{f}(c_8)$	=	(effect	on	financial	ATT	NULL	NULL	NULL)
$\mathbf{f}(c_9)$	=	(on	financial	markets	NULL	NULL	NULL	NULL)
$\mathbf{f}(c_{10})$	=	(financial	markets	.	NULL	NULL	NULL	NULL)
$\mathbf{f}(c_{11})$	=	(on	markets	.	NULL	NULL	ATT	NULL)
$\mathbf{f}(c_{12})$	=	(effect	on	.	ATT	NULL	NULL	ATT)
$\mathbf{f}(c_{13})$	=	(had	effect	.	SBJ	NULL	ATT	ATT)
$\mathbf{f}(c_{14})$	=	(ROOT	had	.	NULL	NULL	SBJ	OBJ)
$\mathbf{f}(c_{15})$	=	(had	.	NULL	SBJ	OBJ	NULL	NULL)
$\mathbf{f}(c_{16})$	=	(ROOT	had	NULL	NULL	NULL	SBJ	PU)
$\mathbf{f}(c_{17})$	=	(NULL	ROOT	NULL	NULL	NULL	NULL	PRED)
$\mathbf{f}(c_{18})$	=	(ROOT	NULL	NULL	NULL	PRED	NULL	NULL)

Figure 3.5: Feature vectors for the configurations in figure 3.2.

Let us now try to put all the pieces together and examine a complete feature representation using only configurational word features. Table 3.1 shows a simple model with seven features, each defined by an address function and an attribute function. We use the notation STK[i] and BUF[i] for the ith word in the stack and in the buffer, respectively,[7] and we use LDEP(w) and RDEP(w) for the farthest child of w to the left and to the right, respectively. The attribute functions used are FORM for word form and DEPREL for dependency label. In figure 3.5, we show how the value of the feature vector changes as we go through the configurations of the transition sequence in figure 3.2.[8]

Although the feature model defined in figure 3.1 is quite sufficient to build a working parser, a more complex model is usually required to achieve good parsing accuracy. To give an idea of the complexity involved, table 3.2 depicts a model that is more representative of state-of-the-art parsing systems. In table 3.2, rows represent address functions, defined using the same operators as in the earlier example, while columns represent attribute functions, which now also include LEMMA (for

---

[7]Note that indexing starts at 0, so that STK[0] is the word on top of the stack, while BUF[0] is the first word in the buffer.
[8]The special value NULL is used to indicate that a feature is undefined in a given configuration.

Table 3.2: Typical feature model for transition-based parsing with rows representing address functions, columns representing attribute functions, and cells with + representing features.

Address	Attributes				
	FORM	LEMMA	POSTAG	FEATS	DEPREL
STK[0]	+	+	+	+	
STK[1]			+		
LDEP(STK[0])					+
RDEP(STK[0])					+
BUF[0]	+	+	+	+	
BUF[1]	+		+		
BUF[2]			+		
BUF[3]			+		
LDEP(BUF[0])					+
RDEP(BUF[0])					+

lemma or base form) and FEATS (for morphosyntactic features in addition to the basic part of speech). Thus, each cell represents a possible feature, obtained by composing the corresponding address function and attribute function, but only cells containing a + sign correspond to features present in the model.

We have focused in this section on configurational word features, i.e., features that can be defined by the composition of an address function and an attribute function, since these are the most important features in transition-based parsing. In principle, however, features can be defined over any properties of a configuration that are believed to be important for predicting the correct transition. One type of feature that has often been used is the *distance* between two words, typically the word on top of the stack and the first word in the input buffer. This can be measured by the number of words intervening, possibly restricted to words of a certain type such as verbs. Another common type of feature is the number of children of a particular word, possibly divided into left children and right children.

3.3.2   TRAINING DATA

Once we have defined our feature representation, we want to learn to predict the correct transition $o(c)$, for any configuration c, given the feature representation $\mathbf{f}(c)$ as input. In machine learning terms, this is a straightforward *classification* problem, where the instances to be classified are (feature representations of) configurations, and the classes are the possible transitions (as defined by the transition system). In a supervised setting, the training data should consist of instances labeled with their correct class, which means that our training instances should have the form $(\mathbf{f}(c), t)$ $(t = o(c))$. However, this is not the form in which training data are directly available to us in a treebank.

In section 2.2, we characterized a training set $\mathcal{D}$ for supervised dependency parsing as consisting of sentences paired with their correct dependency trees:

$$\mathcal{D} = \{(S_d, G_d)\}_{d=0}^{|\mathcal{D}|}$$

In order to train a classifier for transition-based dependency parsing, we must therefore find a way to derive from $\mathcal{D}$ a new training set $\mathcal{D}'$, consisting of configurations paired with their correct transitions:

$$\mathcal{D}' = \{(\mathbf{f}(c_d), t_d)\}_{d=0}^{|\mathcal{D}'|}$$

Here is how we construct $\mathcal{D}'$ given $\mathcal{D}$:

- For every instance $(S_d, G_d) \in \mathcal{D}$, we first construct a transition sequence $C_{0,m}^d = (c_0, c_1, \ldots, c_m)$ such that

    1. $c_0 = c_0(S_d)$,
    2. $G_d = (V_d, A_{c_m})$.

- For every non-terminal configuration $c_i^d \in C_{0,m}^d$, we then add to $\mathcal{D}'$ an instance $(\mathbf{f}(c_i^d), t_i^d)$, where $t_i^d(c_i^d) = c_{i+1}^d$.

This scheme presupposes that, for every sentence S_d with dependency tree G_d, we can construct a transition sequence that results in G_d. Provided that all dependency trees are projective, we can do this using the parsing algorithm defined in section 3.2 and relying on the dependency tree $G_d = (V_d, A_d)$ to compute the oracle function in line 3 as follows:

$$o(c = (\sigma, \beta, A)) = \begin{cases} \text{LEFT-ARC}_r & \text{if } (\beta[0], r, \sigma[0]) \in A_d \\ \text{RIGHT-ARC}_r & \text{if } (\sigma[0], r, \beta[0]) \in A_d \text{ and, for all } w, r', \\ & \text{if } (\beta[0], r', w) \in A_d \text{ then } (\beta[0], r', w) \in A \\ \text{SHIFT}_r & \text{otherwise} \end{cases}$$

The first case states that the correct transition is LEFT-ARC$_r$ if the correct dependency tree has an arc from the first word $\beta[0]$ in the input buffer to the word $\sigma[0]$ on top of the stack with dependency label r. The second case states that the correct transition is RIGHT-ARC$_r$ if the correct dependency tree has an arc from $\sigma[0]$ to $\beta[0]$ with dependency label r – but only if all the outgoing arcs from $\beta[0]$ (according to G_d) have already been added to A. The extra condition is needed because, after the RIGHT-ARC$_r$ transition, the word $\beta[0]$ will no longer be in either the stack or the buffer, which means that it will be impossible to add more arcs involving this word. No corresponding condition is needed for the LEFT-ARC$_r$ case since this will be satisfied automatically as long as the correct dependency tree is projective. The third and final case takes care of all remaining configurations, where SHIFT has to be the correct transition, including the special case where the stack is empty.

3.3.3   CLASSIFIERS

Training a classifier on the set $\mathcal{D}' = \{(\mathbf{f}(c_d), t_d)\}_{d=0}^{|\mathcal{D}'|}$ is a standard problem in machine learning, which can be solved using a variety of different learning algorithms. We will not go into the details of how to do this but limit ourselves to some observations about two of the most popular methods in transition-based dependency parsing: memory-based learning and support vector machines.

Memory-based learning and classification is a so-called lazy learning method, where learning basically consists in storing the training instances while classification is based on similarity-based reasoning (Daelemans and Van den Bosch, 2005). More precisely, classification is achieved by retrieving the k most similar instances from memory, given some similarity metric, and extrapolating the class of a new instance from the classes of the retrieved instances. This is usually called k nearest neighbor classification, which in the simplest case amounts to taking the majority class of the k nearest neighbors although there are a number of different similarity metrics and weighting schemes that can be used to improve performance. Memory-based learning is a purely discriminative learning technique in the sense that it maps input instances to output classes without explicitly computing a probability distribution over outputs or inputs (although it is possible to extract metrics that can be used to estimate probabilities). One advantage of this approach is that it can handle categorical features as well as numerical ones, which means that feature vectors for transition-based parsing can be represented directly as shown in section 3.3.1 above, and that it handles multi-class classification without special techniques. Memory-based classifiers are very efficient to train, since learning only consists in storing the training instances for efficient retrieval. On the other hand, this means that most of the computation must take place at classification time, which can make parsing inefficient, especially with large training sets.

Support vector machines are max-margin linear classifiers, which means that they try to separate the classes in the training data with the widest possible margin (Vapnik, 1995). They are especially powerful in combination with kernel functions, which in essence can be used to transform feature representations to higher dimensionality and thereby achieve both an implicit feature combination and non-linear classification. For transition-based parsing, polynomial kernels of degree 2 or higher are widely used, with the effect that pairs of features in the original feature space are implicitly taken into account. Since support vector machines can only handle numerical features, all categorical features need to be transformed into binary features. That is, a categorical feature with m possible values is replaced with m features with possible values 0 and 1. The categorical feature assuming its ith value is then equivalent to the ith binary feature having the value 1 while all other features have the value 0. In addition, support vector machines only perform binary classification, but there are several techniques for solving the multi-class case. Training can be computationally intensive for support vector machines with polynomial kernels, so for large training sets special techniques often must be used to speed up training. One commonly used technique is to divide the training data into smaller bins based on the value of some (categorical) feature, such as the part of speech of the word on top of the stack. Separate classifiers are trained for each bin, and only one of them is invoked for a given configuration during parsing (depending on the value of the feature

Transition		Preconditions
LEFT-ARC$_r$	$(\sigma\|w_i, w_j\|\beta, A) \Rightarrow (\sigma, w_j\|\beta, A\cup\{(w_j, r, w_i)\})$	$(w_k, r', w_i) \notin A$ $i \neq 0$
RIGHT-ARC$_r$	$(\sigma\|w_i, w_j\|\beta, A) \Rightarrow (\sigma\|w_i\|w_j, \beta, A\cup\{(w_i, r, w_j)\})$	
REDUCE	$(\sigma\|w_i, \beta, A) \Rightarrow (\sigma, \beta, A)$	$(w_k, r', w_i) \in A$
SHIFT	$(\sigma, w_i\|\beta, A) \Rightarrow (\sigma\|w_i, \beta, A)$	

Figure 3.6: Transitions for arc-eager shift-reduce dependency parsing.

used to define the bins). Support vector machines with polynomial kernels currently represent the state of the art in terms of accuracy for transition-based dependency parsing.

3.4   VARIETIES OF TRANSITION-BASED PARSING

So far, we have considered a single transition system, defined in section 3.1, and a single, deterministic parsing algorithm, introduced in section 3.2. However, there are many possible variations on the basic theme of transition-based parsing, obtained by varying the transition system, the parsing algorithm, or both. In addition, there are many possible learning algorithms that can be used to train classifiers, a topic that was touched upon in the previous section. In this section, we will introduce some alternative transition systems (section 3.4.1) and some variations on the basic parsing algorithm (section 3.4.2). Finally, we will discuss how non-projective dependency trees can be processed even if the underlying transition system only derives projective dependency trees (section 3.5).

3.4.1   CHANGING THE TRANSITION SYSTEM

One of the peculiarities of the transition system defined earlier in this chapter is that right dependents cannot be attached to their head until all their dependents have been attached. As a consequence, there may be uncertainty about whether a RIGHT-ARC$_r$ transition is appropriate, even if it is certain that the first word in the input buffer should be a dependent of the word on top of the stack. This problem is eliminated in the *arc-eager* version of this transition system, defined in figure 3.6. In this system, which is called arc-eager because all arcs (whether pointing to the left or to the right) are added as soon as possible, the RIGHT-ARC$_r$ is redefined so that the dependent word w_j is pushed onto the stack (on top of its head w_i), making it possible to add further dependents to this word. In addition, we have to add a new transition REDUCE, which makes it possible to pop the dependent word from the stack at a later point in time, and which has as a precondition that the word on the top of the stack already has a head, i.e., that the arc set contains an arc (w_k, r', w_i) for some k

Transition	Configuration		
	([ROOT],	[Economic, . . . , .],	$\emptyset$)
SH $\Rightarrow$	([ROOT, Economic],	[news, . . . , .],	$\emptyset$)
LA$_{ATT}$ $\Rightarrow$	([ROOT],	[news, . . . , .],	$A_1 = \{$(news, ATT, Economic)$\})$
SH $\Rightarrow$	([ROOT, news],	[had, . . . , .],	A_1)
LA$_{SBJ}$ $\Rightarrow$	([ROOT],	[had, . . . , .],	$A_2 = A_1 \cup \{$(had, SBJ, news)$\})$
RA$_{PRED}$ $\Rightarrow$	([ROOT, had],	[little, . . . , .],	$A_3 = A_2! \cup \{$(ROOT, PRED, had)$\})$
SH $\Rightarrow$	([ROOT, had, little],	[effect, . . . , .],	A_3)
LA$_{ATT}$ $\Rightarrow$	([ROOT, had],	[effect, . . . , .],	$A_4 = A_3 \cup \{$(effect, ATT, little)$\})$
RA$_{OBJ}$ $\Rightarrow$	([ROOT, had, effect],	[on, . . . , .],	$A_5 = A_4 \cup \{$(had, OBJ, effect)$\})$
RA$_{ATT}$ $\Rightarrow$	([ROOT, . . . on],	[financial, markets, .],	$A_6 = A_5 \cup \{$(effect, ATT, on)$\})$
SH $\Rightarrow$	([ROOT, . . . , financial],	[markets, .],	A_6)
LA$_{ATT}$ $\Rightarrow$	([ROOT, . . . on],	[markets, .],	$A_7 = A_6 \cup \{$(markets, ATT, financial)$\})$
RA$_{PC}$ $\Rightarrow$	([ROOT, . . . , markets],	[.],	$A_8 = A_7 \cup \{$(on, PC, markets)$\})$
RE $\Rightarrow$	([ROOT, . . . , on],	[.],	A_8)
RE $\Rightarrow$	([ROOT, . . . , effect],	[.],	A_8)
RE $\Rightarrow$	([ROOT, had],	[.],	A_8)
RA$_{PU}$ $\Rightarrow$	([ROOT, . . . , .],	[ ],	$A_9 = A_8 \cup \{$(had, PU, .)$\})$

Figure 3.7: Arc-eager transition sequence for the English sentence in figure 1.1 (LA$_r$ = LEFT-ARC$_r$, RA$_r$ = RIGHT-ARC$_r$, RE = REDUCE, SH = SHIFT).

and r' (where w_i is the word on top of the stack).[9] To further illustrate the difference between the two systems, figure 3.7 shows the transition sequence needed to parse the sentence in figure 1.1 in the arc-eager system (cf. figure 3.2). Despite the differences, however, both systems are sound and complete with respect to the class of projective dependency trees (or forests that can be turned into trees, to be exact), and both systems have linear time and space complexity when coupled with the deterministic parsing algorithm formulated in section 3.2 (Nivre, 2008). As parsing models, the two systems are therefore equivalent with respect to the Γ and h components but differ with respect to the λ component, since the different transition sets give rise to different parameters that need to be learned from data.

Another kind of variation on the basic transition system is to add transitions that will allow a certain class of non-projective dependencies to be processed. Figure 3.8 shows two such transitions called NP-LEFT$_r$ and NP-RIGHT$_r$, which behave exactly like the ordinary LEFT-ARC$_r$ and RIGHT-ARC$_r$ transitions, except that they apply to the second word from the top of the stack and treat the top word as a context node that is unaffected by the transition. Unless this context node is later attached to the head of the new arc, the resulting tree will be non-projective. Although this system cannot

---

[9]Moreover, we have to add a new precondition to the LEFT-ARC$_r$ transition to prevent that it applies when the word on top of the stack already has a head, a situation that could never arise in the old system. The precondition rules out the existence of an arc (w_k, r', w_i) in the arc set (for any k and r').

Transition		Precondition
NP-Left$_r$	$(\sigma\|w_i\|w_k, w_j\|\beta, A) \Rightarrow (\sigma\|w_k, w_j\|\beta, A \cup \{(w_j, r, w_i)\})$	$i \neq 0$
NP-Right$_r$	$(\sigma\|w_i\|w_k, w_j\|\beta, A) \Rightarrow (\sigma\|w_i, w_k\|\beta, A \cup \{(w_i, r, w_j)\})$	

Figure 3.8: Added transitions for non-projective shift-reduce dependency parsing.

cope with arbitrary non-projective dependency trees, it can process many of the non-projective constructions that occur in natural languages (Attardi, 2006).

In order to construct a transition system that can handle arbitrary non-projective dependency trees, we can modify not only the set of transitions but also the set of configurations. For example, if we define configurations with two stacks instead of one, we can give a transition-based account of the algorithms for dependency parsing discussed by Covington (2001). With an appropriate choice of transitions, we can then define a system that is sound and complete with respect to the class $\mathcal{G}_S$ of arbitrary dependency for a given sentence S. The space complexity for deterministic parsing with an oracle remains $O(n)$ but the time complexity is now $O(n^2)$. To describe this system here would take us too far afield, so the interested reader is referred to Nivre (2008).

3.4.2   CHANGING THE PARSING ALGORITHM

The parsing algorithm described in section 3.2 performs a greedy, deterministic search for the optimal transition sequence, exploring only a single transition sequence and terminating as soon as it reaches a terminal configuration. Given one of the transition systems described so far, this happens after a single left-to-right pass over the words of the input sentence. One alternative to this single-pass strategy is to perform multiple passes over the input while still exploring only a single path through the transition system in each pass. For example, given the transition system defined in section 3.1, we can reinitialize the parser by refilling the buffer with the words that are on the stack in the terminal configuration and keep iterating until there is only a single word on the stack or no new arcs were added during the last iteration. This is essentially the algorithm proposed by Yamada and Matsumoto (2003) and commonly referred to as Yamada's algorithm. In the worst case, this may lead to $n - 1$ passes over the input, each pass taking $O(n)$ time, which means that the total running time is $O(n^2)$, although the worst case almost never occurs in practice.

Another variation on the basic parsing algorithm is to relax the assumption of determinism and to explore more than one transition sequence in a single pass. The most straightforward way of doing this is to use *beam search*, that is, to retain the k most promising partial transition sequences after each transition step. This requires that we have a way of scoring and ranking all the possible transitions out of a given configuration, which means that learning can no longer be reduced to a pure classification problem. Moreover, we need a way of combining the scores for individual transitions in such a way that we can compare transition sequences that may or may not be of the same length, which is a non-trivial problem for transition-based dependency parsing. However, as long as the size of the beam is bounded by a constant k, the worst-case running time is still $O(n)$.

3.5   PSEUDO-PROJECTIVE PARSING

Most of the transition systems that are used for classifier-based dependency parsing are restricted to projective dependency trees. This is a serious limitation given that linguistically adequate syntactic representations sometimes require non-projective dependency trees. In this section, we will therefore introduce a complementary technique that allows us to derive non-projective dependency trees even if the underlying transition system is restricted to dependency trees that are strictly projective. This technique, known as *pseudo-projective parsing*, consists of four essential steps:

1. Projectivize dependency trees in the training set while encoding information about necessary transformations in augmented arc labels.

2. Train a projective parser on the transformed training set.

3. Parse new sentences using the projective parser.

4. Deprojectivize the output of the projective parser, using heuristic transformations guided by augmented arc labels.

The first step relies on the fact that it is always possible to transform a non-projective dependency tree into a projective tree by substituting each non-projective arc (w_i, r, w_j) by an arc $(\text{ANC}(w_i), r', w_j)$, where $\text{ANC}(w_i)$ is an ancestor of w_i such that the new arc is projective. In a dependency tree, such an ancestor must always exist since the ROOT node will always satisfy this condition even if no other node does.[10] However, to make a minimal transformation of the non-projective tree, we generally prefer to let $\text{ANC}(w_i)$ be the *nearest* ancestor (from the original head w_i) such that the new arc is projective.

We will illustrate the projectivization transformation with respect to the non-projective dependency tree in figure 2.1, repeated in the top half of figure 3.9. This tree contains two non-projective arcs: *hearing* $\overset{\text{ATT}}{\rightarrow}$ *on* and *scheduled* $\overset{\text{TMP}}{\rightarrow}$ *today*. Hence, it can be projectivized by replacing these arcs with arcs that attach both *on* and *today* to *is*, which in both cases is the head of the original head. However, to indicate that these arcs do not belong to the true, non-projective dependency tree, we modify the arc labels by concatenating them with the label going into the original head: SBJ:ATT and VC:TMP. Generally speaking, a label of the form HEAD:DEP signifies that the dependent has the function DEP and was originally attached to a head with function HEAD. Projectivizing the tree with this type of encoding gives the tree depicted in the bottom half of figure 3.9.

Given that we have projectivized all the dependency trees in the training set, we can train a projective parser as usual. When this parser is used to parse new sentences, it will produce dependency

---

[10]I.e., for any arc (w_0, r, w_j) in a dependency tree, it must be true that $w_0 \rightarrow^* w_k$ for all $0 < k < j$.

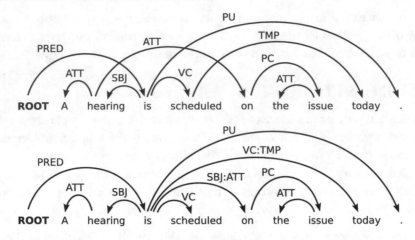

Figure 3.9: Projectivization of a non-projective dependency tree.

trees that are strictly projective as far as the tree structure is concerned, but where arcs that need to be replaced in order to recover the correct non-projective tree are labeled with the special, augmented arc labels. These trees, which are said to be pseudo-projective, can then be transformed into the desired output trees by replacing every arc of the form $(w_i, \text{HEAD:DEP}, w_j)$ by an arc $(\text{DESC}(w_i), \text{DEP}, w_j)$, where $\text{DESC}(w_i)$ is a descendant of w_i with an ingoing arc labeled HEAD. The search for $\text{DESC}(w_i)$ can be made more or less sophisticated, but a simple left-to-right, breadth-first search starting from w_i is usually sufficient to correctly recover more than 90% of all non-projective dependencies found in natural language (Nivre and Nilsson, 2005).

The main advantage of the pseudo-projective technique is that it in principle allows us to parse sentences with arbitrary non-projective dependency trees in linear time, provided that projectivization and deprojectivization can also be performed in linear time. Moreover, as long as the base parser is guaranteed to output a dependency tree (or a dependency forest that can be automatically transformed into a tree), the combined system is sound with respect to the class $\mathcal{G}_S$ of non-projective dependency trees for a given sentence S. However, one drawback of this technique is that it leads to an increase in the number of distinct dependency labels, which may have a negative impact on efficiency both in training and in parsing (Nivre, 2008).

3.6   SUMMARY AND FURTHER READING

In this chapter, we have shown how parsing can be performed as greedy search through a transition system, guided by treebank-induced classifiers. The basic idea underlying this approach can be traced back to the 1980s but was first applied to data-driven dependency parsing by Kudo and Matsumoto (2002), who proposed a system for parsing Japanese, where all dependencies are head-final. The approach was generalized to allow mixed headedness by Yamada and Matsumoto (2003), who applied it to English with state-of-the-art results. The latter system essentially uses the transition system defined in section 3.1, together with an iterative parsing algorithm as described in section 3.4.2, and classifiers trained using support vector machines.

The arc-eager version of the transition system, described in section 3.4.1, was developed independently by Nivre (2003) and used to parse Swedish (Nivre et al., 2004) and English (Nivre and Scholz, 2004) in linear time using the deterministic, single-pass algorithm formulated in section 3.2. An in-depth description of this system, sometimes referred to as Nivre's algorithm, can be found in Nivre (2006b) and a large-scale evaluation, using data from ten different languages, in Nivre et al. (2007). Early versions of this system used memory-based learning but more accurate parsing has later been achieved using support vector machines (Nivre et al., 2006).

A transition system that can handle restricted forms of non-projectivity while preserving the linear time complexity of deterministic parsing was first proposed by Attardi (2006), who extended the system of Yamada and Matsumoto and combined it with several different machine learning algorithms including memory-based learning and logistic regression. The pseudo-projective parsing technique was first described by Nivre and Nilsson (2005) but is inspired by earlier work in grammar-based parsing by Kahane et al. (1998). Systems that can handle arbitrary non-projective trees, inspired by the algorithms originally described by Covington (2001), have recently been explored by Nivre (2006a, 2007).

Transition-based parsing using different forms of beam search, rather than purely deterministic parsing, has been investigated by Johansson and Nugues (2006, 2007b), Titov and Henderson (2007a,b), and Duan et al. (2007), among others, while Cheng et al. (2005) and Hall et al. (2006) have compared the performance of different machine learning algorithms for transition-based parsing. A general framework for the analysis of transition-based dependency-based parsing, with proofs of soundness, completeness and complexity for several of the systems treated in this chapter (as well as experimental results) can be found in Nivre (2008).

CHAPTER 4

Graph-Based Parsing

Well-formed dependency graphs are directed trees that span all the words of the sentence and originate out of the sentence's unique root. Researchers in graph theory have developed a wide range of algorithms for processing both directed and undirected graphs, some of which are the oldest and most well understood in computer science. This raises a question: Is it possible to create dependency parsers that use standard algorithms for directed graphs and trees? This is the basic research question that has been asked in *graph-based* models of dependency parsing, which will be introduced in this chapter. Unlike transition-based systems, a graph-based system explicitly parameterizes models over substructures of a dependency tree, instead of indirect parameterization over transitions used to construct a tree. These models come with many pros and cons relative to their transition-based counterparts, which is a topic that will be addressed in chapter 7. Using our standard conventions, we will define graph-based parsing systems through a model $M = (\Gamma, \boldsymbol{\lambda}, h)$ consisting of a set of constraints on permissible structures Γ, a set of parameters $\boldsymbol{\lambda}$, and a fixed parsing algorithm h. As in the previous chapter, we focus exclusively on systems that do not make use of a formal grammar, thus Γ is simply the set of constraints that force the model to produce a well-formed dependency graph, i.e., a dependency tree.

At the heart of graph-based parsing systems is the notion of the *score* of a dependency tree $G = (V, A) \in \mathcal{G}_S$ for a sentence S:

$$\text{score}(G) = \text{score}(V, A) \in \mathbb{R}$$

This score represents how likely it is that a particular tree is the correct analysis for S. Scores are general and different graph-based systems make different assumptions about how scores are generated. For example, some systems assume that scores are restricted to linear classifiers whereas other systems constrain scores to be conditional or joint probabilities. The fundamental property of graph-based parsing systems is that this score is assumed to factor through the scores of subgraphs of G:

$$\text{score}(G) = f(\psi_1, \psi_2, \ldots, \psi_q) \text{ for all } \psi_i \in \Psi_G$$

Here f is some function over subgraphs ψ and Ψ_G represents the relevant set of subgraphs of G. The nature of f is general, but for most of this chapter we will assume that it is equivalent to a summation over factor parameters and that the score can be rewritten as:

$$\text{score}(G) = \sum_{\psi \in \Psi_G} \lambda_\psi$$

Parameters are constrained to be real values, though their actual make-up is typically more complex such as combinations of weighted feature functions that return real values. Models that sum factor parameters represent the majority of graph-based dependency parsers, but defining the score to be the product of factor parameters is also common (see section 4.1 for more on this).

Using this general blueprint, we can state that any graph-based parsing system must define four things:

1. The definition of Ψ_G for a given dependency tree G.

2. The definition of the parameters $\boldsymbol{\lambda} = \{\lambda_\psi \mid \text{for all } \psi \in \Psi_G, \text{ for all } G \in \mathcal{G}_S, \text{ for all } S\}$.

3. A method for learning $\boldsymbol{\lambda}$ from labeled data.

4. A parsing algorithm $h(S, \Gamma, \boldsymbol{\lambda}) = \text{argmax}_{G \in \mathcal{G}_S} \text{score}(G)$.

The parameter set $\boldsymbol{\lambda}$ appears infinite as it ranges over all possible subgraphs of all dependency trees for all sentences. However, as stated earlier, λ_ψ, is typically not a single variable, but a function that maps subgraphs to real values. Thus, graph-based parsing systems do not store an infinite number of parameters, but instead a finite number of functions over subgraphs. It is only for notational simplicity that we treat these functions as single parameters in the discussion.

This chapter begins with the formulation of the simplest and most common instantiation of graph-based dependency parsing – called *arc-factored* parsing. Detailed parsing algorithms for both projective and non-projective trees are given. We will then discuss common feature representations of these models as well as different learning paradigms used in data-driven implementations. Next, we look at many of the computational difficulties that arise when extending graph-based models beyond arc-factored systems. We conclude with a brief summary and literature overview for further reading.

4.1   ARC-FACTORED MODELS

The smallest and most basic parameterization is over single dependency arcs themselves – the so called *arc-factored models*. Using the above notation we can define arc-factored models for a given dependency tree $G = (V, A)$ as follows:

- $\Psi_G = A$

- $\lambda_\psi = \lambda_{(w_i, r, w_j)} \in \mathbb{R}$ for each $(w_i, r, w_j) \in A$

Thus, in arc-factored models a system assigns a real valued parameter to every labeled arc in the tree. $\boldsymbol{\lambda}$ is thus the set of all arc weights. Precise definitions of $\lambda_{(w_i, r, w_j)}$ will be discussed in section 4.3. We abuse notation here since an arc is not technically a subgraph of G. Instead we let the arc represent the subgraph induced by it, i.e., the subgraph consisting of the two nodes in the arc plus the labeled arc itself.

The score of a dependency tree $G = (V, A)$ is subsequently defined as:

$$\text{score}(G) = \sum_{(w_i, r, w_j) \in A} \lambda_{(w_i, r, w_j)}$$

That is, the score of a tree factors by the parameters of its arcs. Assuming we have access to a meaningful set of parameters λ, then the primary problem of interest is the parsing problem for an arbitrary input S:

$$h(S, \Gamma, \lambda) = \underset{G=(V,A)\in\mathcal{G}_S}{\operatorname{argmax}} \operatorname{score}(G) = \underset{G=(V,A)\in\mathcal{G}_S}{\operatorname{argmax}} \sum_{(w_i,r,w_j)\in A} \lambda_{(w_i,r,w_j)}$$

To solve the parsing problem, an algorithm must find the tree whose component arc parameters sum to the maximum value. In some cases, $\lambda_{(w_i,r,w_j)}$ may represent probabilities or non-negative arc potentials, in which case it would be more natural to multiply arc parameters instead of summing them. However, we can always transform the argmax of a product to an argmax of a summation through a log transform:

$$
\begin{aligned}
h(S, \Gamma, \lambda) &= \underset{G=(V,A)\in\mathcal{G}_S}{\operatorname{argmax}} \prod_{(w_i,r,w_j)\in A} \lambda_{(w_i,r,w_j)} \\
&= \underset{G=(V,A)\in\mathcal{G}_S}{\operatorname{argmax}} \log[\prod_{(w_i,r,w_j)\in A} \lambda_{(w_i,r,w_j)}] \\
&= \underset{G=(V,A)\in\mathcal{G}_S}{\operatorname{argmax}} \sum_{(w_i,r,w_j)\in A} \log \lambda_{(w_i,r,w_j)}
\end{aligned}
$$

Any algorithms we develop for the summation of parameters will naturally extend to a product of parameters by simply re-setting $\lambda_{(w_i,r,w_j)} \equiv \log \lambda_{(w_i,r,w_j)}$.

Our parsing model $M = (\Gamma, \lambda, h)$ is thus a set of constraints Γ restricting valid outputs to dependency trees, a set of arc parameters λ and a parsing function h that solves the above argmax problem. For the moment, we will assume that a meaningful set of parameters is provided to the system and focus our attention on algorithms for computing h. Section 4.3 will examine common paradigms for defining and learning λ.

4.2   ARC-FACTORED PARSING ALGORITHMS

Arc-factored parsing algorithms are based on a straight-forward mapping between dependency trees and the graph-theoretic concept of spanning trees. Let $G = (V, A)$ be a standard directed graph (digraph) or multi-directed graph (multi-digraph) in the case where one allows multiple arcs between nodes. Assume also that there is some scoring function that assigns real values to the arcs in G and the score of any subgraph of G is equal to the sum of its arc scores.

Definition 4.1.   A *maximum spanning tree* or *MST* of a digraph (or a multi-digraph) G is the highest scoring subgraph G' that satisfies the following *spanning tree* conditions:

- $V' = V$, i.e., G' spans all the original nodes in G

- G' is a directed tree

It is not difficult to see how one can define a construction that equates arc-factored dependency parsing to finding the MST of a graph. For an input sentence $S = w_0 w_1 \ldots w_n$, with label set $R = \{r_1, \ldots, r_m\}$ and parameters λ, consider a graph $G_S = (V_S, A_S)$ such that:

- $V_S = \{w_0, w_1, \ldots, w_n\}$ (which is the standard definition of V_S)

- $A_S = \{(w_i, r, w_j) \mid \text{for all } w_i, w_j \in V_S \text{ and } r \in R, \text{ where } j \neq 0\}$

First, note the G_S is a multi-digraph as, for any two nodes w_i and w_j, there are multiple arcs between them – namely one for each possible dependency type r. Second, note that G_S is a complete graph in the node set $V_S - \{w_0\}$ and that there is an arc from w_0 to all other words in the sentence. This definition leads to the following proposition:

Proposition 4.2.   *The set of well-formed dependency graphs (dependency trees) of S, G_S, and the set of spanning trees of G_S are identical.*

Proof. The proof is trivial and falls out of the definition of spanning trees and dependency trees. First, note that any spanning tree of G_S must have as its root w_0 as there are no incoming arcs to it in the graph. Now, any spanning tree originating out of the root word w_0 is by definition a dependency tree (a directed tree spanning all words and rooted at w_0). Furthermore, every valid dependency graph must be a spanning tree of G_S since G_S contains all permissible arcs and a well-formed dependency graph is spanning over the node set V_S and is a directed tree.   □

This simple proposition results in the central corollary for arc-factored models:

Corollary 4.3.   *For an input sentence $S = w_0 w_1 \ldots w_n$, the parsing problem (i.e., solving h) is equivalent to finding the maximum spanning tree of G_S using arc parameters $\lambda_{(w_i, r, w_j)}$.*

Proof. Proposition 4.2 and the fact that dependency trees and spanning trees are both scored by summing arc parameters.   □

Thus, finding the maximum spanning tree of G_S also solves the arc-factored dependency parsing problem. This is only true for the case when we do not include a projectivity constraint on the set G_S as spanning trees can be both projective and non-projective with respect to a sentence S. In fact, algorithms for projective arc-factored parsing do not trace their roots to graph-theoretic algorithms, but instead to chart-parsing algorithms used for parsing context-free grammars. We will examine algorithms for both the non-projective and projective dependency parsing problems as their algorithmic differences will be important when moving beyond arc-factored models.

4.2.1 REDUCING LABELED TO UNLABELED PARSING

In graph-based dependency parsing, we are typically dealing with multi-digraphs since dependency relations are labeled with types. However, for simplicity of presentation we often wish to compute properties only over digraphs, which represents an unlabeled parsing problem. Fortunately, we can proceed with a trivial reduction from labeled parsing to unlabeled parsing, which will result in graphs with a single arc between two nodes. For an input sentence S, and its corresponding multi-digraph G_S, define a new digraph $G'_S = (V'_S, A'_S)$ such that:

- $V'_S = V_S$

- $A'_S = \{(w_i, w_j) \mid w_i, w_j \in V'_S, \text{where } j \neq 0\}$

G'_S is also a complete digraph, but with a single arc between each node. Let us now define a new parameter set over digraph arcs:

$$\lambda_{(w_i, w_j)} = \max_r \lambda_{(w_i, r, w_j)}$$

This reduction from G_S to G'_S and from labeled to unlabeled parameters takes $O(|R|n^2)$ since the new graph G'_S has $O(n^2)$ arcs and the parameter for each arc is determined by enumerating $|R|$ possibilities.

Proposition 4.4. *Let $G = (V, A)$ be the MST of G_S and let $G' = (V', A')$ be the MST of G'_S. The following holds:*

$$(1) \qquad \sum_{(w_i, r, w_j) \in A} \lambda_{(w_i, r, w_j)} = \sum_{(w_i, w_j) \in A'} \lambda_{(w_i, w_j)}$$

$$(2) \qquad (w_i, r, w_j) \in A \quad \text{if and only if} \quad (w_i, w_j) \in A' \text{ and } r = \operatorname*{argmax}_r \lambda_{(w_i, r, w_j)}$$

Proof. If $(w_i, r, w_j) \in A$, then it must be true that $r = \operatorname{argmax}_r \lambda_{(w_i, r, w_j)}$, otherwise we could simply replace this arc with the argmax and get a higher weighted tree. Since we set $\lambda_{(w_i, w_j)}$ to precisely this value, we ensure that the max over the digraph is equivalent to the max over the multi-digraph, making the above equivalences true. We omit the case when two or more labels satisfy $\operatorname{argmax}_r \lambda_{(w_i, r, w_j)}$ since it is trivial to deal with such ties by arbitrarily choosing one label. $\square$

Proposition 4.4 tells us that we can solve the labeled dependency parsing problem by solving the corresponding unlabeled dependency parsing problem – assuming we maintain a reverse map that specifies the original labeled arc from which each unlabeled arc was derived. In sections 4.2.2 and 4.2.3, we will focus on solving the unlabeled parsing problem with the knowledge that this reduction equates it to the original labeled problem of interest.

4.2.2   NON-PROJECTIVE PARSING ALGORITHMS

Dependency parsing algorithms are designated as *non-projective* if their search space $\mathcal{G}_S$ consists of all projective and non-projective dependency trees. From the previous section, we know that it is possible to find the highest scoring dependency tree in this set by finding the maximum spanning tree of G_S. The most common algorithm for finding the MST of a graph is the Chu-Liu-Edmonds algorithm, which is sketched in figure 4.1. The algorithm can be characterized as both *greedy* and *recursive* as it consists of a greedy arc selection step, possibly followed by a recursive call on a transformation of the original complete graph G_S. In the following section, we present an informal analysis of this algorithm and its use in dependency parsing.

Possibly the best way to explore the Chu-Liu-Edmonds algorithm is through an example. We will use the simple sentence $S = $ *John saw Mary* with the induced digraph G_S shown in figure 4.2. This figure will serve to illustrate each step of the algorithm on G_S. Note that we artificially set $\lambda_{(w_j, w_0)} = -\infty$ and disregard these arcs since they should never occur in any well-formed tree. The first step of the main procedure in the algorithm (denoted Chu-Liu-Edmonds in figure 4.1) is to find, for each node, the incoming arc with highest value, which transforms the graph from figure 4.2a to figure 4.2b. If the result of this greedy stage is a tree, it must be an MST and, thus, the most likely dependency tree. To see this, consider a tree constructed by greedily choosing the incoming arc of highest value for every word. Now assume, there exists a different tree with a higher score. Find a node w_j, such that (w_i, w_j) is part of the tree resulting from the greedy arc selection, $(w_{i'}, w_j)$ is part of the hypothesized higher scoring tree, and $i \neq i'$. We know by the definition of the greedy tree that $\lambda_{(w_i, w_j)}$ is at least as large as $\lambda_{(w_{i'}, w_j)}$, so we can simply add (w_i, w_j) to the hypothesized higher scoring tree and subtract $(w_{i'}, w_j)$, and we will obtain a graph (not necessarily a tree) with at least as high a score. If we repeat this process, we will eventually converge to the original tree obtained through greedy arc selection and are always guaranteed that the resulting graph will have a score at least as large as the hypothesized higher scoring tree. Thus, such a higher scoring tree cannot exist and we must have the MST (or one of many MSTs in the case of ties).

However, in the current example, there is a cycle. The Chu-Liu-Edmonds algorithm dictates that we contract this cycle into a single node and recalculate arc parameters according to lines 3 and 4 of the `contract` procedure in figure 4.1. In cases where multiple cycles occur, one can be chosen arbitrarily for contraction. This results in the graph in figure 4.2c. The new node w_{js} represents the contraction of nodes *John* and *saw*. The arc parameter from w_{js} to *Mary* is set to 30 since that is the highest scoring arc from any node in w_{js}. The arc parameter from ROOT into w_{js} is set to 40 since this represents the score of the best spanning tree originating from ROOT and including the nodes in the cycle represented by w_{js}. The same leads to the arc from *Mary* to w_{js}. The fundamental property of the Chu-Liu-Edmonds algorithm is that an MST in this graph can be transformed into an MST in the original graph. This fact follows from a lemma stating that after the greedy step, all but one of the arcs of any cycle must exist in some MST (a single arc must be removed to break the cycle and for the graph to be a tree). Knowing this, we can observe that in the contracted graph, the parameters for arcs going into the contracted node equal the highest score of an arc entering the

Chu-Liu-Edmonds(G, λ)
        Graph $G = (V, A)$
        Arc parameters $\lambda_{(w_i, w_j)} \in \lambda$
1     $A' = \{(w_i, w_j) \mid w_j \in V, w_i = \text{argmax}_{w_i} \lambda_{(w_i, w_j)}\}$
2     $G' = (V, A')$
3   If G' has no cycles, then return G' and quit
4   Find any arc set A_C that is a cycle in G'
5     $< G_C, w_c, ep > = \text{contract}(G', A_C, \lambda)$
6     $G = (A, V) = \text{Chu-Liu-Edmonds}(G_C, \lambda)$
7   For the arc $(w_i, w_c) \in A$ where $ep(w_i, w_c) = w_j$,
        identify the arc $(w_k, w_j) \in C$ for some w_k
8   Find all arcs $(w_c, w_l) \subset A$
9     $A = A \cup \{(ep(w_c, w_l), w_l)\}_{\text{for all } (w_c, w_l) \in A}$
         $\cup A_C \cup \{(w_i, w_j)\} - \{(w_k, w_j)\}$
10   $V = V$
11   return G

h(S, Γ, λ) – non-projective
        Sentence $S = w_0 w_1 \ldots w_n$
        Arc parameters $\lambda_{(w_i, w_j)} \in \lambda$
1   Construct $G_S = (V_S, A_S)$
        $V_S = \{w_0, w_1, \ldots, w_n\}$
        $A_S = \{(w_i, w_j) \mid \text{for all } w_i, w_j \in V_S\}$
2   return Chu-Liu-Edmonds(G_S, λ)

contract$(G = (V, A), C, \lambda)$
1   Let G_C be the subgraph of G excluding nodes in C
2   Add a node w_c to G_C representing cycle C
3   For $w_j \in V - C : \exists_{w_i \in C}(w_i, w_j) \in A$
     Add arc (w_c, w_j) to G_C with
        $ep(w_c, w_j) = \text{argmax}_{w_i \in C} \lambda_{(w_i, w_j)}$
        $w_i = ep(w_c, w_j)$
        $\lambda_{(w_c, w_j)} = \lambda_{(w_i, w_j)}$
4   For $w_i \in V - C : \exists_{w_j \in C}(w_i, w_j) \in A$
     Add arc (w_i, w_c) to G_C with
        $ep(w_i, w_c) = \text{argmax}_{w_j \in C} \left[\lambda_{(w_i, w_j)} - \lambda_{(a(w_j), w_j)}\right]$
        $w_j = ep(w_i, w_c)$
        $\lambda_{(w_i, w_c)} = \left[\lambda_{(w_i, w_j)} - \lambda_{(a(w_j), w_j)} + \text{score}(C)\right]$
        where $a(w)$ is the predecessor of w in C
        and $\text{score}(C) = \sum_{w \in C} \lambda_{(a(w), w)}$
5   return $< G_C, w_c, ep >$

Figure 4.1: The Chu-Liu-Edmonds spanning tree algorithm for non-projective dependency parsing.

cycle and breaking it, e.g., the arc parameter from ROOT into w_{js} is 40 representing that arc entering the node *saw* and breaking the cycle by removing the single arc from *John* to *saw*.

    The algorithm is then recursively called (steps c to d in figure 4.2). Note that one must keep track of the real endpoints of the arcs into and out of w_{js} for reconstruction later. This is done through the function *ep* in figure 4.1. Running the greedy step in this case results in a tree and therefore the MST of this graph. The algorithm concludes by traversing up a recursive call to reconstruct the dependency tree. The arc from w_{js} to *Mary* originally was from the node *saw*, so that arc is included.

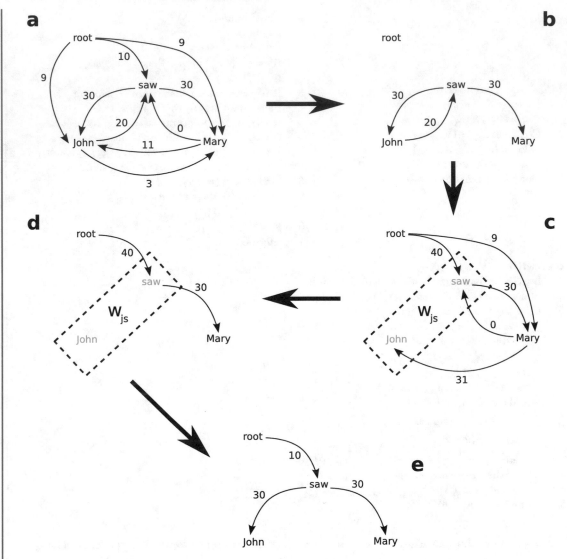

Figure 4.2: The Chu-Liu-Edmonds algorithm illustrated on an example English sentence *John saw Mary*.

Furthermore, the arc from ROOT to w_{js} represented a tree from ROOT to *saw* to *John*, so all those arcs are included to get the final (and correct) MST.

Naively, this algorithm runs in $O(n^3)$ time since each recursive call takes $O(n^2)$ to find the highest incoming arc for each word and to identify a cycle and contract the graph. Furthermore, there are at most n recursive calls since we cannot contract the graph more than n times as each contraction ultimately results in a smaller graph. An improvement to $O(n^2)$ was given by Tarjan (1977) for complete/dense graphs, which is precisely what we need here. We omit discussion of the Tarjan implementation since it only complicates matters and, in practice, the simpler $O(n^3)$ algorithm above rarely requires n recursive calls. Once we take into account the $O(|R|n^2)$ time to reduce the labeled multi-digraph to a digraph, then the resulting run-time for finding the MST is at worst $O(|R|n^2 + n^2) = O(|R|n^2)$.

4.2.3   PROJECTIVE PARSING ALGORITHMS

The set of *projective* dependency trees is equivalent to the set of *nested* dependency trees under the assumption of an artificial root node as the leftmost word. As such, it is well-known that projective dependency parsers are strongly related to context-free parsers. The result of this equivalence means that many standard algorithms for parsing context-free grammars can be altered to parse projective dependency trees. In particular, a simple variant of the Cocke-Kasami-Younger (CKY) algorithm for context-free parsing serves the purpose. Alternative methods for projective dependency parsing that embed dependency arcs directly into a CFG are explored in chapter 5.

To start, we will define a dynamic programming table, denoted by $C[s][t][i]$, which represents the value of the highest scoring projective tree that spans the string $w_s \ldots w_t$ and which is rooted at word w_i, where $s \leq i \leq t$. For convenience, we graphically represent a table entry $C[s][t][i]$ through a labeled triangle, as in figure 4.3e. Clearly, if we could populate C, then $C[0][n][0]$ would represent the highest scoring dependency tree for an input sentence $S = w_0 w_1 \ldots w_n$, which is precisely the value we are interested in for the parsing problem. The question then becomes how to fill the table. The base case is trivial:

$$C[i][i][i] = 0.0, \text{ for all } 0 \leq i \leq n$$

This is because any dependency tree of a single word must have a score of 0 as there are no dependency arcs to contribute. Now, assume that $C[s][t][i]$ is correctly populated for all s, t and i such that $s \leq i \leq t$ and $0 \leq t - s \leq n'$, for some $n' < n$. Let us now attempt to fill an entry in the table $C[s][t][i]$, where $t - s = n' + 1$. First, we note that any projective tree rooted at w_i and spanning w_s to w_t is ultimately made up of smaller adjacent subgraphs (as shown in figure 4.3a). Secondly, we note that larger trees may be constructed by continuously adding adjacent dependency arcs from the inside out, creating subgraphs spanning larger and larger strings until the last subgraph is added, as illustrated in figure 4.3a-e.[1] Thus, to build a subgraph that spans w_s to w_t, we only need to consider the final merger of two subtrees as all other subtree constructions are accounted for in our hypothesis about C for smaller spans where $t - s \leq n'$. This observation is identical to that made by context-free parsing algorithms. The possible dependency arc and subtree merges we must consider

---

[1]Typically, a pre-specified order is used, such as all dependencies to the left are first created before all to the right. This is required when spurious ambiguity in parse derivations must be avoided.

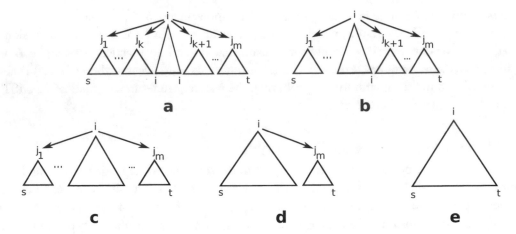

Figure 4.3: Illustration showing that every projective subgraph can be broken into a combination of smaller adjacent subgraphs.

for calculating $C[s][t][i]$ are given in figure 4.4, and we can write the corresponding recurrence:

$$C[s][t][i] = \max_{s \le q < t, s \le j \le t} \begin{cases} C[s][q][i] + C[q+1][t][j] + \lambda_{(w_i, w_j)} & \text{if } j > i \\ C[s][q][j] + C[q+1][t][i] + \lambda_{(w_i, w_j)} & \text{if } j < i \end{cases} \qquad (4.1)$$

That is, we need to consider all possible dependents of w_i, call them w_j, and all possible substring spans, indexed by q. A simple structural induction proof can be given for the correctness of this algorithm by noting that the base case of span length 0 holds and our inductive hypothesis shows that, for any length span, we can correctly calculate C assuming C has been computed for all shorter spans. After C is populated, $C[0][n][0]$ will be the entry of interest since it corresponds to the highest weighted tree spanning all words and rooted at w_0. A simple bottom-up algorithm based on CKY can be constructed around this recurrence to fill in C. This algorithm starts by filling out the base case of span size 1 ($t - s = 0$), and then uses the recurrence to fill out all entries of the table where $t - s = 1$, then all entries where $t - s = 2$, etc. This algorithm will run in $O(n^5)$ since it must fill $O(n^3)$ entries in the table, and each entry must consider $O(n^2)$ possibilities, i.e., the maximum over q and j. When we add the $O(|R|n^2)$ factor to reduce the parsing problem from the labeled case to the unlabeled case, the total run-time is $O(|R|n^2 + n^5)$.

The above algorithm simply finds the score of the best tree and does not define a mechanism for extracting this tree. This can be done in a number of ways. Perhaps the easiest is to maintain an auxiliary arc table, $A[s][t][i]$, which is populated parallel to C and contains all the arcs in the highest scoring tree spanning w_s to w_t rooted at w_i. In equation 4.1, we already found the maximum q and j for populating $C[s][t][i]$. We can simply use these two indices to define a recurrence for $A[s][t][i]$

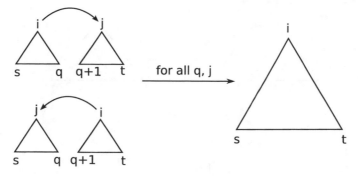

Figure 4.4: CKY algorithm for projective dependency parsing.

as:

$$A[i][i][i] = \{\}$$

$$A[s][t][i] = \begin{cases} A[s][q][i] \cup A[q+1][t][j] \cup (w_i, w_j) & \text{if } j > i \\ A[s][q][j] \cup A[q+1][t][i] \cup (w_i, w_j) & \text{if } j < i \end{cases}$$

The final tree for a sentence S is then $G = (V, A[0][n][0])$. This technique only adds at most $O(n)$ when computing the inner loop since there can never be more than n arcs in a well-formed graph. Since the inner loop is already $O(n^2)$ due to the search for q and j, maintaining $A[s][t][i]$ does not change the run-time complexity of CKY. However, the space complexity is now $O(n^4)$ as opposed to $O(n^3)$ when we just had to maintain C. A more space efficient method of tree reconstruction is to use back-pointers – a technique common in inference algorithms that are based on Viterbi's algorithm, of which CKY and the present projective dependency parsing algorithm can be viewed as generalizations to trees. In the back-pointer method, instead of storing an entire graph $A[s][t][i]$, each entry instead stores the two indices, q and j, making the size of the table $O(n^3)$. These indices are then used to reconstruct the graph recursively starting at entry $A[0][n][0]$.

Any parsing algorithm that runs in $O(n^5)$ is unlikely to be much use in practical situations without heavy pruning or approximations. Fortunately, Eisner's algorithm for projective dependency parsing provides a straight-forward technique for reducing the runtime complexity substantially. This comes from a simple observation that a word w_i may collect its left dependents independent of its right dependents without any global repercussions in finding the highest weighted tree. Consider the tree in figure 4.3a. A parsing algorithm can first construct two separate subgraphs, one spanning from w_i to w_t and another spanning from w_s to w_i, each representing the right or left dependents of w_i respectively. Note that in both these subgraphs, the head of the tree w_i is at the periphery. Let us use this observation to break apart the construction of a dependency arc into smaller but equivalent steps. Graphically, this can be seen in figure 4.5 in which every item has the head of the subgraph at the periphery. Briefly, Eisner's algorithm starts by considering the left and right subgraphs of the

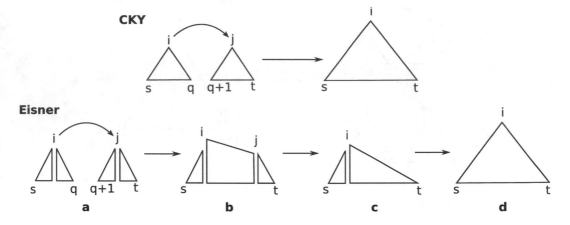

Figure 4.5: Illustration showing Eisner's projective dependency parsing algorithm relative to CKY.

original trees headed by w_i and w_j. A dependency arc is then created from w_i to w_j (step a to b). This creates a new type of subgraph that is headed by w_i and contains *only* the left subgraph headed by w_j. This intermediate type of subgraph is required since it constrains the next step to subsume w_j's right subgraph and maintain equivalence with the original $O(n^5)$ algorithm. This is precisely what happens in the next stage when we transition from step b to step c. Finally, we can combine the left and right subgraphs rooted at w_i to recover the equivalent outcome as the $O(n^5)$ algorithm (step d). This last step is merely to give the reader an intuition of the equivalence between the two algorithms, and in fact is never needed.

At first, it may appear that breaking each arc construction into smaller steps has made things worse. However, we can note that every subgraph in figure 4.5a-c only requires indices for two words: the head, which is now at the periphery, and the opposite peripheral index. Consider a dynamic programming table of the form $E[s][t][d][c]$, which is intended to represent the highest weighted subgraph spanning w_s to w_t, with head either w_s (when $d = 1$) or w_t (when $d = 0$). Additionally, c indicates whether the subgraph is constrained only to consider left/right subgraphs of the dependent in the previous arc construction ($c = 1$) or not ($c = 0$). Graphically, all possibilities are outlined in figure 4.6. Using the simple breakdown of CKY given in figure 4.5, we can then define a new dynamic programming algorithm to populate E. We call this algorithm *Eisner's algorithm*. Pseudo-code for filling the dynamic programming table is in figure 4.7.

The algorithm begins by first initializing all length-one subgraphs to a weight of 0.0, just as in CKY. Then, the algorithm considers spans of increasing length. In the inner loop, the first step is to construct new dependency arcs, i.e., steps a-b in figure 4.5. This is done by taking the max over all internal indices in the span, $s \leq q < t$, and calculating the value of merging the two subgraphs and adding the corresponding arc. For reference, line 8 is equivalent to step a to step b in figure 4.5. Line 7 is the symmetric case of a left dependency arc. After new arcs are added, the algorithm attempts

$$E[s][t][0][0] \qquad E[s][t][1][0] \qquad E[s][t][0][1] \qquad E[s][t][1][1]$$

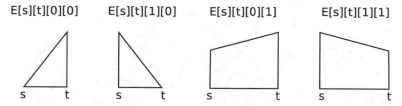

Figure 4.6: Illustration showing each type of subgraph in the dynamic program table used in Eisner's algorithm.

Eisner(S, Γ, λ)

      Sentence $S = w_0 w_1 \ldots w_n$

      Arc weight parameters $\lambda_{(w_i, w_j)} \in \lambda$

1   Instantiate $E[n][n][2][2] \in \mathbb{R}$

2   Initialization: $E[s][s][d][c] = 0.0 \quad$ for all s, d, c

3   for $m : 1..n$

4   for $s : 1..n$

5        $t = s + m$

6   if $t > n$ then break

       % Create subgraphs with $c = 1$ by adding arcs (step a-b in figure 4.5)

7        $E[s][t][0][1] = \max_{s \leq q < t} \ (E[s][q][1][0] + E[q+1][t][0][0] + \lambda_{(w_t, w_s)})$

8        $E[s][t][1][1] = \max_{s \leq q < t} \ (E[s][q][1][0] + E[q+1][t][0][0] + \lambda_{(w_s, w_t)})$

       % Add corresponding left/right subgraphs (step b-c in figure 4.5)

9        $E[s][t][0][0] = \max_{s \leq q < t} \ (E[s][q][0][0] + E[q][t][0][1])$

10      $E[s][t][1][0] = \max_{s < q \leq t} \ (E[s][q][1][1] + E[q][t][1][0])$

Figure 4.7: Pseudo-code for Eisner's algorithm.

to add corresponding left/right subgraphs to arcs that have been previously added (either in the last step, or for smaller length substrings). A simple proof by structural induction shows that this algorithm considers all possible subgraphs and, as a result, $E[s][t][d][c]$ is correct for all values of the four index variables. We can then take $E[0][n][1][0]$ as the score of the best dependency tree. Additionally, we can use an auxiliary arc table or back-pointers to reconstruct this tree, as is done for CKY.

    In terms of complexity, Eisner's algorithm is $O(n^3)$. The table $E[s][t][d][c]$ is $O(n^2 \times 2 \times 2) = O(n^2)$ in size. To fill each entry, we must consider $O(n)$ possibilities, i.e., the max over q in all lines of the inner loop figure 4.7. When we add on the $O(|R|n^2)$ runtime for reducing the labeled

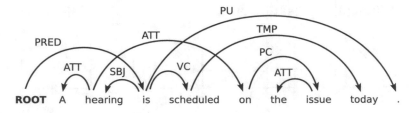

Figure 4.8: Non-projective dependency tree for an English sentence.

parsing problem to the unlabeled parsing problem, the final runtime is $O(|R|n^2 + n^3)$, which is a substantial improvement over using an $O(|R|n^2 + n^5)$ CKY style algorithm. In addition to running proportional to $O(n^3)$, Eisner's algorithm is based on bottom-up dynamic programming techniques, which, as we will later show, provides additional benefits when moving beyond arc-factored parsing models.

4.3 LEARNING ARC-FACTORED MODELS

In chapter 2, we defined a data-driven dependency parsing model $M = (\Gamma, \boldsymbol{\lambda}, h)$ as containing both a set of parameters $\boldsymbol{\lambda}$ and a parsing algorithm h. To this point, we have defined the general form of the parameters as factoring over arcs in a tree, as well as resulting parsing algorithms that find the highest scoring tree given the parameters. However, we have yet to discuss the specific form of each arc parameter $\lambda_{(w_i, r, w_j)}$ and how the parameters can be learned from an annotated data set.

4.3.1 PARAMETER AND FEATURE REPRESENTATIONS

Graph-based parsing systems typically assume that the arc parameters are linear classifiers between a vector of pre-defined features over the arc $\mathbf{f}(w_i, r, w_j) \in \mathbb{R}^m$ and a corresponding feature weight vector $\mathbf{w} \in \mathbb{R}^m$,

$$\lambda_{(w_i, r, w_j)} = \mathbf{w} \cdot \mathbf{f}(w_i, r, w_j)$$

The arc feature function $\mathbf{f}$ can include any relevant feature over the arc or the input sentence S. Features are typically categorical and post-hoc converted to binary features. For example, let us consider the arc (hearing, ATT, on) from figure 4.8 (reproduced from chapter 2). A feature representation might consist of the following categorical features (each feature is shown with the value it takes on for figure 4.8):

- Identity of w_i = *hearing*

- Identity of w_j = *on*

- Identity of part-of-speech tag for w_i = NN

- Identity of part-of-speech tag for w_j = IN

- Identity of r = ATT

- Identity of part-of-speech tags between w_i and w_j = VBZ, VBN

- Identity of part-of-speech tag for w_{i-1} = DT

- Identity of part-of-speech tag for w_{i+1} = VBZ

- Identity of part-of-speech tag for w_{j-1} = VBN

- Identity of part-of-speech tag for w_{j+1} = DT

- Distance (in number of words) between w_i and w_j = 2

- Direction of arc = RIGHT

These features can then be combined to create even more complex categorical features such as,

- Identity of w_i = *hearing* & Identity of w_j = *on* & Direction of arc = RIGHT

For highly inflected languages, additional features could cover a morphological analysis of the words to promote agreement in gender, number, and other properties. Categorical features like those above are translated into real-valued features through binarization, as was the case for categorical features in transition-based systems. For a categorical feature with m possible values, we create m different features in **f** with values of 0 or 1 to indicate the absence or presence of the feature-value pair. The fact that most features in **f** will have values of 0 permits the use of sparse representations and calculations.

This brief section is meant to give the reader a flavor of the kinds of features used in today's graph-based dependency parsing systems. Of course, larger and more sophisticated feature sets do exist, and we point the reader to the relevant literature in section 4.5.

4.3.2 TRAINING DATA

We assume that a learning algorithm has access to a training set,

$$\mathcal{D} = \{(S_d, G_d)\}_{d=1}^{|\mathcal{D}|}$$

of input sentences S_d and corresponding dependency trees G_d. In chapter 3, a transformation from dependency trees to a sequence of parser configurations and transitions was required in order to train classifiers to assume the part of the oracle. For graph-based systems, things are much simpler. Since we have parameterized the models directly over the trees, there is no need to transform the training data. All learning algorithms described in this section assume that the training data are in the form given above.

4.3.3   LEARNING THE PARAMETERS

As we have already defined efficient algorithms for finding the most likely dependency tree, a common learning technique for graph-based dependency parsing is *inference-based learning*. Under the assumption that arc parameters are linear classifiers, the inference problem, embodied in the function h, is:

$$h(S, \Gamma, \boldsymbol{\lambda}) = \underset{G=(V,A)\in\mathcal{G}_S}{\operatorname{argmax}} \sum_{(w_i,r,w_j)\in A} \lambda_{(w_i,r,w_j)} = \underset{G=(V,A)\in\mathcal{G}_S}{\operatorname{argmax}} \sum_{(w_i,r,w_j)\in A} \mathbf{w}\cdot\mathbf{f}(w_i, r, w_j)$$

In this setting, $\boldsymbol{\lambda}$ contains both the learned weight vector $\mathbf{w}$ and the predefined feature function $\mathbf{f}$. For simplicity we will focus on the one of the simplest and most common inference-based learning algorithms, the perceptron algorithm. Pseudo-code for the algorithm is given in figure 4.9. The perceptron algorithm builds a linear classifier online by considering a single training instance in isolation, finding the highest weighted tree (i.e., solving h in line 4), and then adding weight to features that are present in the correct solution while subtracting weight from features that are present in a possibly incorrect solution. When the data is linearly separable, the perceptron algorithm is guaranteed to find a $\mathbf{w}$ that classifies $\mathcal{D}$ perfectly.[2] Crucially, the perceptron algorithm only relies on the solution to h (line 4), which we already have defined in this chapter. Thus, if we define a set of relevant features, then an inference-based learning algorithm like the perceptron can be employed to induce a meaningful set of parameters $\boldsymbol{\lambda}$ from a training set $\mathcal{D}$. Though many graph-based parsing systems rely only on inference and associated inference-based learning algorithms, there are many other possibilities that arise naturally out of the arc-factored framework. These include probabilistic log-linear models, large-margin models, and generative bigram models. Many of these learning algorithms require computations beyond inference, most notably the summation of tree scores over the set $\mathcal{G}_S$ or expected values of arcs under a probabilistic model. These computations can be more expensive and complex than the Chu-Liu-Edmonds algorithm. Pointers to work in this area are provided in section 4.5.

4.4   BEYOND ARC-FACTORED MODELS

This chapter has so far been devoted to arc-factored models for graph-based dependency parsing. This is for many good reasons: Arc-factored models are conceptually simple, based on well known algorithms from graph-theory, language independent (outside any specific definition of $\boldsymbol{\lambda}$ and $\mathbf{f}$), and produce state-of-the-art parsing systems. Though arc-factored models are appealing computationally, they are not justified linguistically as their underlying arc independence assumption is simply not valid. Dependencies in any syntactic structure depend on one another, often in complex ways. In this section, we explore what happens when we move beyond arc-factored models. We look at two simple extensions. The first is to introduce the notion of arity into the parameters, which will measure how likely a given word is to have a fixed number of dependents. The second extension

---

[2]Collins (2002) provides a more detailed analysis including proofs of convergence and bounds on generalization error.

Perceptron($\mathcal{D}$)

    Training data $\mathcal{D} = \{(S_d, G_d)\}_{d=1}^{|\mathcal{D}|}$

1    $\mathbf{w} = \mathbf{0}$

2   for $n : 1..N$

3   for $d : 1..|\mathcal{D}|$

4   Let $G' = h(S_d, \Gamma, \boldsymbol{\lambda}) = \text{argmax}_{G' \in \mathcal{G}_{S_d}} \sum_{(w_i, r, w_j) \in A'} \mathbf{w} \cdot \mathbf{f}(w_i, r, w_j)$

5   if $G' \neq G_d$

6           $\mathbf{w} = \mathbf{w} + \sum_{(w_i, r, w_j) \in A_d} \mathbf{f}(w_i, r, w_j) - \sum_{(w_i, r, w_j) \in A'} \mathbf{f}(w_i, r, w_j)$

7   return $\mathbf{w}$

Arc parameters can then be calculated: $\lambda_{(w_i, r, w_j)} = \mathbf{w} \cdot \mathbf{f}(w_i, r, w_j)$

Figure 4.9: The perceptron learning algorithm as used in graph-based dependency parsing.

increases the scope of factorization and introduces model parameters over two or more neighboring arcs in the tree. In both cases, it can be shown that non-projective parsing becomes computationally intractable. In contrast, projective parsing remains feasible through simple augmentations to the CKY reduction described above.

The *arity* of a word w_i in a sentence is the number of dependents it has in the correct dependency tree, denoted a_{w_i}. For instance, the word *had* in figure 1.1 has an arity of 3, whereas the word *effect* has an arity of 2. Arity is a useful parameter when considering the score of a dependency tree, e.g., a verb should have an arity greater than zero, whereas an article most likely will have an arity of zero. Our parameters should attempt to capture this fact. To do this, we first define a_{w_i} as the arity of w_i in a graph G. Next, we add an additional parameter to the standard arc-factored model, $\lambda_{a_{w_i}}$, that measures the likelihood of a word having a particular arity α. The score of a tree $G = (V, A)$ is now defined as:

$$\text{score}(G) = \sum_{(w_i, r, w_j) \in A} \lambda_{(w_i, r, w_j)} + \sum_{w_i \in V} \lambda_{a_{w_i}}$$

We do not weight the terms in this sum as any weighting can easily be folded into the parameters.

Notice that this additional parameter directly ties together the previously independent arcs since it introduces an implicit trade-off in the parameters controlling arity and the parameters that create each arc. It is not difficult to show that this simple augmentation results in non-projective parsing becoming intractable. Consider the NP-complete problem of finding a Hamiltonian Path in a digraph. As input, the system is given a connected digraph and, as output, the system must indicate whether there exists at least one directed path that includes all nodes of the graph with no cycles. For an arbitrary digraph $G = (V, A)$, we can reduce the Hamiltonian Path problem for G by defining a sentence $S = w_0 v_1 \ldots v_n$, for all $v_i \in V$ and a new word w_0. We then define the parameters as follows: $\lambda_{(w_0, -, v_i)} = 0$; $\lambda_{(v_i, -, v_j)} = 0$ iff $(v_i, v_j) \in A$; $\lambda_{a_{w_0}=1} = 0$; $\lambda_{a_{v_i}=1} = 0$; and $\lambda_{a_{v_i}=0} = 0$. All other parameters are set to $-\infty$. Note that we omit arc labels as they are not needed in the reduction.

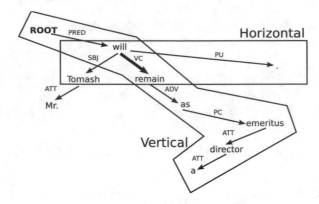

Figure 4.10: Horizontal and vertical Markov neighborhoods for the arc (will, VC, remain).

It is straightforward to show that the highest scoring dependency tree for S has a score of 0 if and only if there exists a Hamiltonian path for G. This is because the arity constraints force each node to have an arity of at most 1 or suffer a $-\infty$ parameter in the summation. As a result, any dependency tree must be just a single path connecting all nodes. Furthermore, the arity parameters, as well as the well-formed dependency graph definition, are defined so that the only node that can be the root is w_0, so we can just remove that node and recover the path. It is also straightforward to see that any Hamiltonian path corresponds to a zero scoring dependency tree (just add an arc from w_0 to the root of the path). Thus, if we could solve the parsing with arity problem tractably, then we would have an efficient solution for the Hamiltonian path problem, which cannot be true unless $P = NP$. Of course, this is just a worst-case analysis and says nothing about the average-case or situations where strong assumptions are made about the distribution of parameter values.

The second extension beyond arc-factored models we consider is Markovization. In general, we would like to say that every dependency decision is dependent on every other arc in a tree. However, modeling all dependencies simultaneously is clearly not computationally feasible. Instead, it is common to approximate this by making a Markov assumption over the arcs of the tree, in a similar way that a Markov assumption can be made for sequential classification problems like part-of-speech tagging with a hidden Markov model. Markovization can take two forms for dependency parsing: horizontal or vertical relative to some arc (w_i, r, w_j), and we denote each as the horizontal and vertical *neighborhoods* of (w_i, r, w_j), respectively. The vertical neighborhood includes all arcs in any path from ROOT to a leaf that passes through (w_i, r, w_j). The horizontal neighborhood contains all arcs (w_i, r', w'_j). Figure 4.10 graphically displays the vertical and horizontal neighborhoods for the arc (will, VC, remain).

Vertical and horizontal Markovization essentially allow the score of the tree to factor over a large scope of arcs, provided that they are in the same vertical or horizontal neighborhood. A dth order factorization is one in which the score of a tree factors only over d arcs – the arc itself plus the nearest $d - 1$ arcs in a neighborhood (arc-factored models are equivalent to $d = 1$). It turns out, that even for 2nd order factorizations, non-projective parsing is intractable. As a result, all higher orders of factorization are intractable since a dth factorization can always be embedded in a $d + 1^{st}$ factorization by ignoring any additional arcs. We start by looking at the horizontal case. Mathematically, a 2nd order horizontal Markovization will have parameters for every pair of adjacent arcs in a tree. Let us define a new parameter $\lambda_{(w_i,r,w_j)(w_i,r',w'_j)}$ that parameterizes two horizontally adjacent arcs with head word w_i. The score of a tree can then be defined as:

$$\text{score}(G = (V, A)) = \sum_{(w_i,r,w_j),(w_i,r',w'_j) \in A} \lambda_{(w_i,r,w_j)(w_i,r',w'_j)} + \sum_{(w_i,r,w_j) \in A} \lambda_{(w_i,r',w_j)}$$

where the first summation is constrained to consider only adjacent arcs in the same horizontal neighborhood. We have also included the original arc-factored parameters to account for head words with an arity of 1. This is a notational convenience as these parameters can be folded into the 2nd order parameters.

Consider the NP-complete problem of 3-dimensional matching (3DM). As input, we are given three sets of size m, call them A, B and C, and a set $T \subset A \times B \times C$. The 3DM problem asks whether there is a set $T' \subseteq T$ such that $|T'| = m$ and for any two tuples (a, b, c), $(a', b', c') \in T'$, it is the case that $a \neq a'$, $b \neq b'$, and $c \neq c'$. There is a simple reduction from 3DM to the parsing problem with horizontal Markovization. We first define a new input sentence $S = w_0 a_1 \ldots a_m b_1 \ldots b_m c_1 \ldots c_m$. Next, we set the parameters $\lambda_{(a_i,-,b_j),(a_i,-,c_k)} = 1$, $\lambda_{(a_i,-,b_j)} = 0$, and $\lambda_{(a_i,-,c_k)} = 0$ if and only if $(a_i, b_j, c_k) \in T$. We again omit arc labels since they are not needed. We additionally set $\lambda_{(w_0,-,a_i),(w_0,-,a_j)} = 0$, $\lambda_{(w_0,-,a_i)} = 0$ for all $a_i, a_j \in A$. All other parameters are set to $-\infty$. The key is that there is a 3DM if and only if the highest scoring dependency tree has a score of m. First, no dependency tree can have a score greater than m. Second, the only trees with a score of m will be those that contain arcs from w_0 to all a_i (contributes zero to the overall score), and each a_i will have exactly two outgoing arcs to a pair b_j, and c_k (there must be m of these and the horizontal parameters will each contribute a value of one to the score). Any such tree represents a 3DM since each a, b, and c, will be involved in exactly one pair of arcs $(a, -, b)$ and $(a, -, c)$ representing the matching. Conversely, all valid matchings are trees with scores of m under the definition of the parameters. Thus, there exists a 3DM if and only if the highest scoring dependency tree has a score of m. As a result, the parsing problem with horizontal Markovization is unlikely to be tractable. The vertical case can also be shown to be NP hard using a similar reduction from 3DM where one ties the vertical arc parameters to items in the set T.

Arity and Markovization represent two of the simplest means of extending graph-based models beyond arc-factored assumptions. Even these small extensions result in a loss of computational efficiency and provide strong evidence that any extension that ties together the construction of more than one arc is unlikely to be feasible. This is a strongly negative result as most linguistic theories tell us that strong independence assumptions between dependencies are not well-founded. Such considerations have led to a line of research exploring approximations and guided brute-force techniques to produce non-projective parsing systems without arc-factored

The above discussion does not assume any projectivity constraints and holds for the non-projective case only. Once we assume projectivity, moving beyond arc-factored models is straight-forward. This is because the dynamic programming tables at the heart of projective algorithms can be easily augmented to account for non-local information. For simplicity, let us consider the $O(n^5)$ CKY style parsing algorithm and the entry $C[s][t][i]$ of the dynamic programming table, which is shown graphically below:

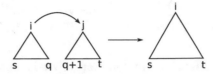

In this case, the algorithm iterates over all q and j, finding the maximum of the subtree scores plus the parameter for the new arc from w_i to w_j (we omit the symmetric case where $i > j$). To account for arity, we can simply augment the chart to $C[s][t][i][\alpha]$, where α represents the arity of the root w_i of the subtree spanning w_s to w_t. The algorithms main recurrence can then be written as:

$$C[i][i][i][\alpha] = \begin{cases} 0 & \text{if } \alpha = 0 \\ -\infty & \text{otherwise} \end{cases}$$

$$C[s][t][i][\alpha] = \max_{s \leq q < t, s \leq j \leq t, \alpha'} \begin{cases} C[s][q][i][\alpha - 1] + C[q + 1][t][j][\alpha'] & \text{if } j > i \\ \quad + \lambda_{(w_i, w_j)} + (\lambda_{a_{w_i} = \alpha} - \lambda_{a_{w_i} = \alpha - 1}) \\ \\ C[s][q][j][\alpha'] + C[q + 1][t][i][\alpha - 1] & \text{if } j < i \\ \quad + \lambda_{(w_i, w_j)} + (\lambda_{a_{w_i} = \alpha} - \lambda_{a_{w_i} = \alpha - 1}) \end{cases}$$

Note that we have to subtract out the old arity parameter for w_i and replace it with the new arity of α. The highest scoring tree is then:

$$\underset{\alpha > 0}{\text{argmax}} \ C[0][n][0][\alpha]$$

The recurrence requires an additional iteration over the arity of w_j, which results in a new runtime of $O(n^6)$ since α can potentially take n different values. This is a simple worst-case analysis only meant to show that the run-time is polynomial in n.

Polynomial algorithms are also easily constructed for both horizontal and vertical Markoviza-tion. In these cases, the dynamic programming table is again augmented, but with information of neighboring arcs, e.g., the most previous left (or right) dependent that w_i subsumed, or the head of w_i. The recurrences can similarly be augmented to ensure that the table is filled correctly.

4.5   SUMMARY AND FURTHER READING

In this chapter we have discussed various properties of graph-based parsing systems. This included an in-depth look at arc-factored models, the most common graph-based instantiation, as well as the computational implications of extensions beyond them. We discussed both projective and non-projective parsing algorithms and saw that, for arc-factored models, projective algorithms are less efficient in the worst-case ($O(n^3)$ relative to $O(n^2)$ for non-projective algorithms). However, once we move beyond arc-factored models, projective parsing easily remains polynomial in the length of the input sentence, whereas non-projective parsing becomes intractable. This difference opens many new directions of research. Clearly, the bottom-up dynamic programming backbone of projective algorithms allows them to be augmented to move beyond arc-factored assumptions. Do bottom-up algorithms exist for finding non-projective trees? Most likely not, otherwise we should be able to augment them in similar ways to get efficient non-projective algorithms without arc-factored assumptions. Do they exist for a subset of non-projective structures? How linguistically plausible is this subset? If they exist, what is their relationship to other formalisms like tree adjoining grammars and combinatorial categorial grammars (Bodirsky et al., 2005; Kuhlmann and Möhl, 2007). The fact that graph-based non-projective parsing becomes intractable when moving beyond arc-factored models is related to the work of Neuhaus and Bröker (1997). In that work, it was shown that parsing in any grammar-based model satisfying some minimal conditions must be NP hard. One of these conditions was that the grammar models arity.

Before we finish this chapter, it is worthwhile mentioning some of the literature available for the interested reader. Graph-based methods can be traced to the mid 1990s in the work of Eisner (1996b) who proposed a generative model of dependency parsing and the cubic parsing algorithm described here. Though not explicitly called graph-based, Eisner's work could be viewed abstractly as 2nd order horizontal graph-based parsing. Roughly ten years after the initial work of Eisner, extensive work began on discriminative methods for training graph-based dependency parsers pioneered by McDonald, Crammer and Pereira (2005). It was in this and subsequent work that the use of graph-theoretic algorithms for dependency parsing began to be explored thoroughly.

In terms of parsing algorithms, Eisner's projective algorithm has been used in Eisner (1996b,a); Paskin (2001, 2002); McDonald, Crammer and Pereira (2005); McDonald and Pereira (2006); McDonald (2006). Context-free parsing algorithms that form the basis for the projective parsing algorithms described in this chapter include the CKY algorithm (Younger, 1967) and Earley's algorithm (Earley, 1970). The Chu-Liu-Edmonds algorithm is described formally in Chu and Liu (1965); Edmonds (1967); Tarjan (1977); Georgiadis (2003), and was first used in dependency parsing systems by Ribarov (2004) and McDonald, Pereira, Ribarov and Hajič (2005). A k-best extension for the Chu-Liu-Edmonds is described in Camerini et al. (1980) and was used in the re-ranking model of Hall (2007). Both non-projective and projective algorithms borrow techniques from sequential processing including the use of back-pointers from the Viterbi algorithm (Viterbi, 1967; Rabiner, 1989) and Markovization (Rabiner, 1989).

Many learning methods for arc-factored dependency parsing have been proposed, including perceptron-based methods (McDonald, Crammer and Pereira, 2005; McDonald, Pereira, Ribarov and Hajič, 2005; McDonald and Pereira, 2006; Corston-Oliver et al., 2006; Carreras, 2007), probabilistic models both generative (Eisner, 1996b; Paskin, 2001; Klein and Manning, 2002; McDonald and Satta, 2007; Wallach et al., 2008) and discriminative (Hall, 2007; Koo et al., 2007; Nakagawa, 2007; Smith and Smith, 2007), and max-margin methods (Koo et al., 2007). Probabilistic or other models that require computing the sum of tree scores or arc expectations use the matrix-tree theorem (Tutte, 1984) for non-projective parsing, the application of which was explored in Koo et al. (2007), McDonald and Satta (2007), and Smith and Smith (2007). Paskin (2001) studied probabilistic models for projective trees, in which inside-outside like algorithms (Lari and Young, 1990) can be used. Models that move beyond arc-factored assumptions include approximations based on projective algorithms (McDonald and Pereira, 2006; McDonald et al., 2006), re-ranking methods using k-best algorithms (Hall, 2007), integer linear programming techniques (Riedel and Clarke, 2006), branch-and-bound algorithms (Hirakawa, 2006), sampling methods (Nakagawa, 2007), belief propagation (Smith and Eisner, 2008), and tractable projective extensions for Markovization (Eisner, 1996b; McDonald and Pereira, 2006; Carreras, 2007).

Different feature sets have been explored including those for arc-factored models (McDonald, Crammer and Pereira, 2005) as well as for non-arc-factored models (McDonald and Pereira, 2006; Hall, 2007; Carreras, 2007; Nakagawa, 2007). McDonald (2006) explores the impact on parsing accuracy of various feature sets.

There have also been studies using graph-based inference algorithms for voting over the outputs of different parsing systems (Sagae and Lavie, 2006). These methods usually define $\lambda_{(w_i, r, w_j)}$ as the number of different parsers that predicted that arc. With these parameters, Eisner's algorithm or the Chu-Liu-Edmonds algorithm can then be used to produce the tree that, on average, has the most frequently predicted arcs across all different parsers.

CHAPTER 5

Grammar-Based Parsing

In this chapter, we introduce grammar-based methods for dependency parsing. In contrast to the data-driven methods treated in chapters 3 and 4, grammar-based methods rely on an explicitly defined formal grammar. As a consequence, we have a more restrictive definition of the parsing model, $M = (\Gamma, \lambda, h)$. In the previous chapters, we defined Γ as a set of constraints. In this chapter, we will assume that it represents a well-defined formal grammar. In such approaches, parsing is defined as the analysis of a sentence with respect to the given grammar and a parameter set, $G = h(S, \Gamma, \lambda)$. As a consequence, if the parser finds an analysis, the sentence is said to belong to the language described by the grammar. If the parser does not find an analysis, the sentence does not belong to the language.

In purely grammar-based approaches, the parameter set λ is typically empty. Exceptions can be found in approaches in which probabilities for grammar rules are learned, in which case the set consists of the learned probabilities, or approaches that use weighted constraints. For the latter case, the parameter set can be determined manually or acquired automatically. If the parameter set is learned, the resulting parsing algorithm is an example of a combination of grammar-based and data-driven parsing.

The first approach that we will discuss here can be described as a modification of constituent-based parsing methods, in which a context-free grammar is used (section 5.1). This method represents dependencies as production rules in a context-free grammar. In this way, standard chart parsing methods can be used. In section 5.1.1, we will investigate a conversion of a dependency grammar into an efficiently parsable context-free grammar as well as probability models that can be used for parsing such projective grammars.

The second approach to grammar-based dependency parsing that we discuss defines dependency parsing as a constraint satisfaction problem (section 5.2). Here, the grammar consists of a set of constraints that restrict possible analyses. Since constraint resolution in the general case is NP complete, the parser must employ a heuristic to guarantee that a locally optimal analysis is found efficiently. In such approaches, the constraints are generally written manually.

Definition 5.1. A *grammar* Γ of language L for our purposes is any formal, finite-size, complete description of L.

This definition is out of necessity rather vague because the grammars used in the two approaches discussed here are very different. We will define these grammars in more detail in the respective sections. The definition of grammar also has a reverse side that concerns the set of sentences that are accepted by the grammar. That is, if a sentence is not accepted by the grammar, it is not part of the language. This is in contrast to strictly data-driven approaches where even non-standard sentences

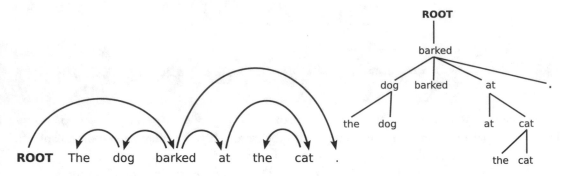

Figure 5.1: Short dependency example and its representation as a context free tree structure.

are intended to be analyzed as completely as possible. This may be intended in robust systems, where a wrong or partial analysis is generally preferred to complete failure, or it may be a consequence of the setup, which is the case for the data-driven parsers presented in the previous chapters.

5.1 CONTEXT-FREE DEPENDENCY GRAMMAR

In section 4.2.3, we looked at projective dependency parsing from a graph-theoretic viewpoint. Here, we will use the same parsing method, but we will concentrate on the formal grammar aspect.

A projective dependency grammar can be viewed as a special case of a context-free grammar in which the non-terminal symbols are words. Thus, the dependency representation in figure 5.1 is a tree structure analysis, which implicitly represents a context-free grammar. In this case, the head and its immediate dependents constitute a constituent in which the word that is the head also serves as the head of the constituent. The root of the tree is the ROOT of the dependency tree. We have restricted this example to dependencies without labels since the approaches which we explore in this section are cleaner to present without them. However, the models described in this section can easily be extended to include labels by augmenting words. In the example in figure 5.1, the word *the*, for example, could be extended to *the:ATT*, specifying that the word is in an ATT-relation to its head.

Definition 5.2. A *context-free grammar* Γ is a 4-tuple (N, Σ, Π, START) where

1. N is a finite set of non-terminal symbols,

2. Σ is a finite set of terminal symbols,

3. Π is a set of production rules of the form $X \rightarrow \alpha$ (where $X \in N$ is a (single) non-terminal symbol, and α is string of non-terminal and terminal symbols),

4. START $\in N$ is the start symbol.

In the case of a context-free dependency grammar, N contains one non-terminal symbol for every word in Σ. Because of this correspondence, we can represent the non-terminals by the words, as we have done in figure 5.1. START is ROOT, α is a string of words, and X consists of the head of this string. Thus, each node in the tree structure is lexicalized in the sense of being labeled with a terminal symbol. This leads to a considerably higher number of nonterminal symbols in comparison to traditional context-free grammars.

The advantage of regarding a dependency grammar as a context-free grammar is that all the well-studied parsing algorithms for such grammars, for example CKY (Younger, 1967) or Earley's algorithm (Earley, 1970), can be used for dependency parsing as well. A parsing algorithm that is especially adapted to dependency parsing (Eisner's algorithm) was introduced in section 4.2.3. Note that non-projective dependencies cannot be dealt with in this approach.

In the following section, we will look at ways of converting dependency grammars into efficiently parsable context-free grammars and discuss probability models that can be used in conjunction with such grammars. One improvement for the standard CKY parsing algorithm was presented in section 4.2.3. This algorithm can be used in grammar-based parsing as well. In this case, the grammar is either written manually or extracted from a treebank. However, the grammar needs to be in the form of a *bilexical* context-free grammar.

Definition 5.3.   A *bilexical context-free grammar* Γ_B is a context-free grammar in which Π consists of a set L of left dependencies $H \rightarrow NH\ H$ and a set R of right dependencies[1] $H \rightarrow H\ NH$.

Each production rule has two right-hand-side symbols, the head of a constituent H (which is also the left-hand-side node) and a non-head node NH. In such a grammar, all dependents are generated independently inside-out, i.e., the dependents closest to the head are generated first. The resulting tree structure is binary. A tree structure based on a bilexical grammar for the sentence in figure 5.1 is shown in the first tree in figure 5.2. For ease of transition to a more complex conversion, we represent the non-terminals with a lexicalized non-terminal symbol X_h, which expands to w_h and all of its dependents.

Note that bilexical context-free grammars are not equivalent to standard CFGs. In a CFG, it is possible to have constraints on children both to the left and to the right of the head. In bilexical CFGs, this is not possible since the left and right children are generated independently of each other. For more details see Nivre (2002).

5.1.1   PARSING WITH BILEXICAL GRAMMARS

One problem with the conversion presented above concerns the time complexity of a chart parser using a bilexical grammar. Since the parser has to keep track of which word in a constituent is the head (i.e., which word will serve as the left-hand-side node in a production), apart from the other indices in chart parsing, the time complexity is $O(n^3 \cdot \min(|\Pi|, n^2))$. Since there is one non-terminal

---

[1]Note that the R used in these rules as well as in the rest of this section should not be confused with the one used for dependency types in previous chapters.

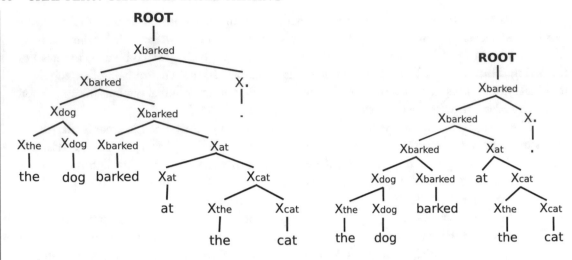

Figure 5.2: Two possible tree structures based on a bilexical grammar.

for every terminal, the number of production rules will in all practical situations be larger than n^2, so the resulting complexity is no better than $O(n^5)$. An additional problem results from the fact that the conversion produces spurious tree structures since the order in which the dependents from the left and right are added is not defined. Figure 5.2 shows two of the possible tree structures for the dependency tree shown in figure 5.1. In order to avoid spurious structures and to reduce complexity to $O(n^3)$, a split-head representation can be used instead.

In a split-head representation, each terminal w_i of the dependency tree is represented as two terminals: w_i^l and w_i^r. The intuition behind this conversion method is to attach all the left dependents of a word to terminal w_i^l and all the right dependents to terminal w_i^r. The introduction of two terminals per word leads to the two lexical rules:

$$L_i^l \rightarrow w_i^l$$
$$R_i^r \rightarrow w_i^r$$

In order to assemble the two terminals (with their dependents), we need the following rule:

$$X_i \rightarrow L_i^l \ R_i^r$$

Additionally, we need the following rules for left ($w_j \leftarrow w_i$) and right ($w_i \rightarrow w_j$) dependencies:

$$L_i \rightarrow X_j \ L_i$$
$$R_i \rightarrow R_i \ X_j$$

Last, we need a rule to create the root node for the dependency ROOT $\rightarrow w_i$:

$$\text{ROOT} \rightarrow X_i$$

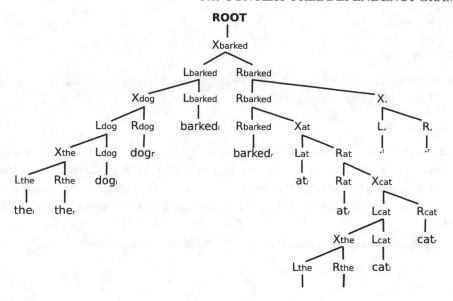

Figure 5.3: The split-head representation of the sentence in figure 5.1.

The split-head context-free tree structure that corresponds to the sentence in figure 5.1 is shown in figure 5.3. Since L_i collects all its left dependents, constituents headed by this symbol will always have the head w_i^l as the rightmost word in the constituent. For this reason, we do not need the indices on L_i and can reduce it to L. For R_i^r, the head is always the leftmost word. However, we do need the index on X_j. Therefore, parsing such structures requires $O(n^4)$ parsing time. A more efficient representation of dependency trees needs to do away with X_j. This can be done with the Unfold-Fold transformation, a method borrowed from functional programming, as described below.

Since we only have one rule with X on the left, we can replace all occurrences of X_j by the two symbols on the right-hand-side of the original rule $X_j \rightarrow L_j^l \ R_j^r$:

$$L_i \rightarrow L_j \ R_j \ L_i$$
$$R_i \rightarrow R_i \ L_j \ R_j$$

Now, we do not need X_j anymore, but instead we have ternary rules, which again results in a parsing time requirement of $O(n^4)$ since more combinations of partial trees are possible. For this reason, we introduce a new symbol, $M_{i,j}$, which groups the original symbol with its neighboring new symbol. This means that in the rule for L_i, we group R_j and L_i; and in the rule for R_i, we group R_i and L_j. Note that the sequence of symbols in both cases is the same, so that we need only one M rule for both cases.

$$L_i \rightarrow L_j \ M_{i,j}$$
$$R_i \rightarrow M_{i,j} \ R_j$$
$$M_{i,j} \rightarrow R_i \ L_j$$

Note also that we do not need the symbol X any longer as we can again replace it in the ROOT rule by the right-hand-side of its original production:

$$\text{ROOT} \rightarrow L_i \ R_i$$

The next question is: What do we gain by replacing X by a new symbol M with two indices? If we look more closely, we see that we do not need the indices at all. We already know that we do not need them for L and R. For $M_{i,j}$, the leftmost word is from its L_i daughter, i.e., w_i, and the rightmost word is from R_j, i.e., w_j. As a consequence, a grammar based on this transformation can be parsed in $O(n^3)$ time.

To wrap up the conversion, here is the complete set of grammar rules:

$$
\begin{aligned}
&\text{ROOT} \rightarrow L_i R_i && \text{for ROOT} \rightarrow w_i \\
&L_i^l \rightarrow w_i^l && \\
&R_i^r \rightarrow w_i^r && \\
&L_i \rightarrow L_j \ M_{i,j} && \text{for } w_j \leftarrow w_i \\
&R_i \rightarrow M_{i,j} \ R_j && \text{for } w_i \rightarrow w_j \\
&M_{i,j} \rightarrow R_i \ L_j && \text{for all } i,j \in \Sigma
\end{aligned}
$$

The tree structure resulting from this conversion for the sentence in figure 5.1 is shown in figure 5.4.

So far, we have discussed an efficient representation for a bilexical grammar, which provides us with a purely grammar-based approach to dependency parsing. In practice, bilexical grammars are often data-driven as they are combined with a set of learned parameters $\boldsymbol{\lambda}$. One possibility would be to use the feature-based arc-factored parameterization presented in section 4.1 and to learn the parameters using the perceptron algorithm. Whereas before we had a direct parameterization over an arc $w_i \rightarrow w_j$, we would now have a parameterization over production rules like $X_i \rightarrow X_i \ X_j$ and $X_i \rightarrow X_j \ X_i$ (or rules like $L_i \rightarrow L_j \ M_{i,j}$ in a transformed grammar). The primary difference is that now we have a formal grammar that can further restrict the space of well-formed dependency trees for a sentence. In fact, if one simply includes all possible productions in the grammar, the two systems would be identical (with the exception that graph-based models can also handle non-projectivity through different parsing algorithms), which again shows that the division between grammar-based and data-driven models is more for illustrative purposes.

However, the fact that it is possible to represent dependency grammars using context-free grammars allows one to employ any number of data-driven techniques that are available for CFGs. Perhaps the simplest is a probabilistic context-free grammar (PCFG). A PCFG is parameterized over productions $X \rightarrow \alpha$ of the grammar, where each parameter is the conditional probability of observing a production rule's right-hand-side given the left-hand-side non-terminal,

$$\lambda_{X \rightarrow \alpha} = P(X \rightarrow \alpha)$$

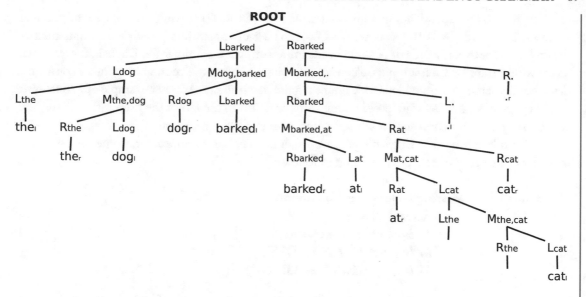

Figure 5.4: Unfold-Fold representation of the sentence in figure 5.1.

$$\text{such that} \sum_{\alpha} \lambda_{X \to \alpha} = \sum_{\alpha} P(X \to \alpha) = 1$$

The parameters of the model can then be set using a variety of methods, the most common of which is to maximize the likelihood of a training set derived from a treebank. In the case of bilexical grammars, each production takes the form $X_i \to X_j \ X_i$ or $X_i \to X_j \ X_i$, making this yet another model that factors over dependency arcs. Models of this form are commonly called *bilexical probability models*, as they model the probability of observing a head-dependent pair in a dependency tree. Just as was the case for projective graph-based parsing systems, it is possible to extend these models to incorporate additional dependency context such as horizontal or vertical dependencies.

5.2 CONSTRAINT DEPENDENCY GRAMMAR

As mentioned previously, a dependency parsing model consists of a grammar, a set of parameters, and a fixed parsing algorithm, $M = (\Gamma, \boldsymbol{\lambda}, h)$. The grammar in the present case is a constraint dependency grammar, and the parsing algorithm is a constraint satisfaction solver (see below for details). The parameters are optional, but they can be present in the form of weights on the constraints (see section 5.2.1 for more details).

A constraint dependency grammar is a triple $\Gamma = (\Sigma, R, C)$ in which Σ is the set of terminal symbols, i.e., words; R is the label set; and C is the set of constraints.[2] Such constraints restrict dependencies between words or possible heads for a word. In a grammar for English, for example, a rule would state that a noun phrase consists of a determiner and a countable noun. A constraint describes the same situation: Countable nouns require determiners. Another example of a constraint would be: Possible heads for prepositions are verbs or nouns to the left of the preposition. Thus, the constraints have a function similar to production rules in a CFG grammar.

The rule stating that English nouns are either mass nouns, require a determiner or a genitive modifier can be formulated as a constraint as follows:

Constraint 5.4.   **Missing Determiner Constraint:**
$$X.cat = \text{NN} \rightarrow$$
1) $has\_feature(X.feat, mass\_noun) \mid$
2) $has\_dependent(X.id, \text{DET}) \mid$
3) $has\_dependent(X.id, \text{GMOD})$

The missing determiner constraint states that each word with the part-of-speech tag NN (normal noun) is either marked as a mass noun or is modified by a determiner (DET) or a genitive modifier (GMOD). In our example, the first line gives the name of the constraint. In the second line, we state the category that is covered by the constraint, i.e., all words with the part-of-speech tag NN. In this constraint, we use a single variable, X. The remaining lines following the right arrow specify the conditions that must hold. In order to specify constraints, we need to specify attributes that can be accessed and functions that check for properties of the word and its attributes. We have access to the word itself (or rather its unique index, to be exact) $X.id$, to its part-of-speech tag $X.cat$, and to its head $X{\uparrow}id$. In our example, we use two functions, $has\_feature$, and $has\_dependent$, which check whether a word has a certain feature or a certain dependent.

In a constraint dependency approach, parsing is defined as a constraint satisfaction problem (CSP). For a fully defined CSP, we need to specify the variables, their domains, and the set of constraints that need to be satisfied:

1. The set of variables $S = w_0 w_1 \ldots w_n$ represents the set of words in the sentence.

2. The domain of the variables w_i is the set $\{w_j \mid 1 \leq j \leq n \text{ and } j \neq i\}$ (the possible heads of a word).

3. The set C of constraints defines the permissible values for variables.

The set of variables corresponds to the words in the sentence, their domain is the set of possible heads, i.e., all other words in the sentence except the word itself. For example, the sentence

---

[2]We can extend this definition to a 4-tuple in which a separate set is included that represents different levels of annotation. For example, we can then distinguish between syntactic and semantic constraints. Since we concentrate on the syntactic level here, the triple suffices.

Economic news had little effect on financial markets.

has the set of variables $S = \{Economic, news, had, little, effect, on, financial, markets\}$, the domain of variable *Economic* is the set $\{news, ..., markets\}$, the domain of *news* is the set $\{Economic, had, ..., markets\}$ if we disregard the period.

Now, methods from constraint satisfaction can be used to solve the parsing problem. Since constraint satisfaction problems in general are NP complete, heuristic search techniques must be used. One possible search technique is constraint propagation, a technique that enforces local consistency. Similar to graph-based parsing, constraint propagation starts by assuming a fully connected graph, a *constraint network*, in which the nodes represent the variables (i.e., the words), and the arcs the constraints. At the beginning, every word hypothetically depends on every other word in the sentence. The constraints are then used to exclude certain dependencies. The constraint that a preposition can only depend on preceding nouns or verbs, for example, excludes all other possibilities. These constraints are then propagated throughout the network, thus deleting inconsistent values. If, after the application of all constraints, there are still variables with more than one possible value, the sentence could not be disambiguated completely by the given set of constraints. In this case, disambiguation can be completed by a variety of techniques or heuristics. One possibility to avoid incompletely resolved parses is the use of weights for the constraints. In this case, violations of constraints with the least important weight are preferred.

5.2.1   WEIGHTED CONSTRAINT DEPENDENCY GRAMMAR

The use of *hard* constraints, i.e., constraints that must always be satisfied, as described above has turned out to be too rigorous an approach. Natural language is characterized by a high degree of exceptions to rules or by phenomena which can more easily be described by preferences rather than by rules. Languages with free word order provide a good reason for using such preferences. In German, for example, there are strict rules for the placement of verbal elements but there is more freedom in the ordering of non-verbal elements. As a consequence, the subject occurs in sentence-initial position only in approximately 50% of the sentences. Another useful application of soft constraints can be found in relative clauses in English. They generally follow the noun phrase that they modify. However, in certain cases, the relative clause can be extraposed. In these cases, the variation can either be permitted by not constraining the phenomenon in question at all or by a weighted constraint so that non-canonical word order results in the violation of a constraint with a low weight. The first option generally results in an increase in ambiguity and is therefore less desirable.

Another problem that is caused by hard constraints concerns robustness issues. Even carefully edited text often contains ungrammatical usages, either by mistake or in word plays. Manually written grammars often cover only grammatical language and thus are unable to provide an analysis for such sentences. Since grammar-based methods assume that the grammar is able to distinguish between grammatical and ungrammatical sentences, it would be counter-productive to include ungrammatical rules or constraints into the grammar. In addition, even if the grammar writer had decided to include such cases, it is difficult to come up with all possible ungrammatical cases. For this reason, *soft* or *defeasible* constraints are used instead. In this approach, each constraint is assigned a weight between 0.0 (= hard constraint) and 1.0. This weight defines the importance of the constraint relative to other constraints. For a constraint c, we denote its weight by the parameter λ_c. The acceptability of an analysis, weight(G), is defined as the product of the weights of all constraints c violated in the analysis:

$$\text{weight}(G) = \prod_{c \in C} \lambda_c$$

An acceptability of 0.0 would indicate ungrammaticality. As a consequence, hard constraints, which must be satisfied, have the weight 0.0. The higher the weight, the more acceptable the violation of the respective constraint. Thus, preferences tend to have scores closer to 1.0. Note that this is counter-intuitive, but in a model in which weights are multiplied, a sentence weight of 0.0 translates into an ungrammatical analysis.

The difference between English and German subject positions can be described by the following weighted constraints:

Constraint 5.5. **English Subject Position : 0.1**
$$X.label = \text{SBJ} \rightarrow distance(X.id, X{\uparrow}id) > 0$$

Constraint 5.6. **German Subject Position : 0.5**
$$X.label = \text{SBJ} \rightarrow distance(X.id, X{\uparrow}id) > 0$$

Here, X refers to the subject, while $X{\uparrow}id$ refers to the head of the subject. Both constraints state, using the distance relation, that the subject is to be found to the left of its head ($X{\uparrow}id$). For English, the weight of the constraint is close to 0.0, indicating that it is a constraint whose violation results in a low acceptability score. For German, in contrast, the weight is higher, thus indicating that the violation of the constraint can still lead to an acceptable analysis. The weights can either be assigned manually, thus leading to a purely grammar-based approach, or they can be learned from a labeled set of data, in which case the resulting constraint dependency grammar is categorized as both a grammar-based and a data-driven approach.

5.2.2 TRANSFORMATION-BASED CONSTRAINT DEPENDENCY PARSING

The method based on constraint propagation and weighted constraints achieves good parsing results. However, it suffers from the following problems: The constraints are often insufficient for reaching a complete disambiguation of a sentence. When this is the case, the solution consists in applying heuristics, which increases the risk that the correct solution will be deleted so that from the remaining variable values, no solution can be reached. For this reason, we will look at an alternative parsing method that is based on repair. The idea underlying this method is to start with an (arbitrary) dependency analysis for a sentence and repair it step by step, guided by the weights of the constraints.

That is, the dependency that violates the constraint with the lowest weight (i.e. the hardest constraint) should be repaired first. Since the resulting dependency tree must be complete, the method has the *anytime property*, i.e., the process can be stopped at any time with a complete analysis.

The design of such a repair method needs to answer the following questions:

1. Which dependency graph should be used as the initial graph?

2. Which variable should be modified next?

3. If a variable w is to be modified, which value should be chosen?

The simplest approach to the question concerning the initial graph assignment is to use a random graph. However, since convergence normally depends on the quality of the initial graph, it is reasonable to choose initial results that optimize unary constraints.

Definition 5.7.   A *unary constraint* is a constraint that restricts the domain of a single variable.

The constraints presented in this section (see, e.g., constraint 5.4) are unary constraints. Since only one variable is involved, unary constraints can be checked very efficiently.

At first glance, there is a very obvious answer to the question of which variable to choose next: Select the violated constraint with the lowest weight and repair it. This process is repeated until there are no more violations. One problem with this approach is that only one constraint violation at a time is repaired. In cases where more than one hard constraint is violated, the repaired graph will still have an acceptability score of 0.0 (since the sentence score is calculated as the product of the constraint weights) and will show no improvement. In order to cover such cases properly, the selection function must separate hard and soft constraints and prefer solutions with fewer violations of hard constraints. Thus, a solution that violates 3 hard constraints is considered better than one that violates 4 hard constraints, independently of how many soft constraints are violated.

Another problem with the approach described so far is that it tends to converge to local maxima. Here, a local maximum is a state in the sequence of repairs in which every possible next repair step results in a deterioration in acceptability, but which may eventually lead to the best solution. If reaching the global optimum requires more than one step, the first of these steps will lead to a deterioration before the global optimum can be reached. Figure 5.5 (adapted from Foth, 1999) shows such a situation for the German sentence *Die Katze jagt der Hund.* (The$_{ACC}$ cat$_{ACC}$ chases the$_{NOM}$ dog$_{NOM}$.). The first graph (a) incorrectly assumes the canonical word order with subject before and direct object after the verb. This analysis violates only the constraint that ensures case agreement in a noun phrase. In order to reach the global optimum (e), the subject and direct object label must exchange places, and the case assignments for *die Katze* and for *der Hund* must be corrected. The resulting graph would only violate the subject position preference, which is a less important violation. However, every single step away from the local maximum leads to lower accuracy. In order to leave the local maximum, the algorithm must be allowed to pursue steps that explore solutions with initially suboptimal scores. For the example in figure 5.5, first, the agreement violation between

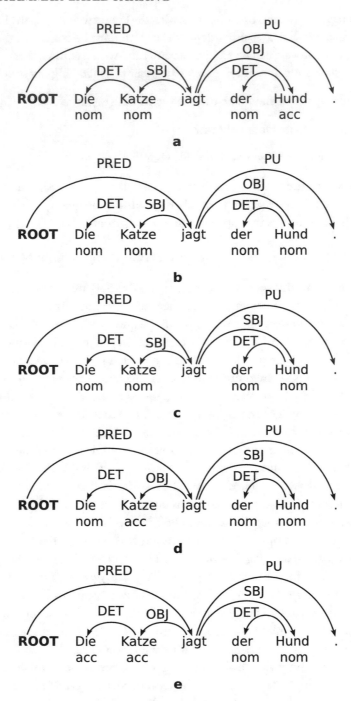

Figure 5.5: A local minimum reached by the repair method (a) and the steps to the global optimum (e).

der and *Hund* is corrected so that the determiner is marked as being nominative (b). This correction leads to the violation of the constraint that requires a direct object to be in accusative. This violation is remedied by making *Hund* the subject of the sentence (c). Then *Katze* cannot be the subject and is thus changed to direct object (d). Finally, both *die* and *Katze* must change their case annotation to accusative (e). This analysis only violates the preference for having the subject in first position, which is a softer constraint than the case agreement constraint so that the resulting analysis is the global optimum.

However, one problem is that there is no guarantee that a better solution will be found when sub-optimal steps are explored. For this reason, and in order to ensure the anytime property of the algorithm, the previously found optimal solution (which may still be a local maximum) is stored in memory so that it can be retrieved when the search is stopped without finding a better solution. Another problem is that allowing the algorithm to pursue suboptimal solutions by randomly selecting violations to correct may result in a cycle. Thus, after the first suboptimal repair step in the example above, the algorithm has the choice between correcting the object agreement violation and undoing the modification and going back to the local maximum. While the latter improves the overall score, the former results in a further deterioration. In order to avoid such circular behavior, the algorithm must keep track of which constraint violations have already been corrected. These violations cannot be repeated. Such a guided search is called *tabu search* Glover and Laguna (1977). After a further modification of the algorithm, the resulting transformation-based constraint dependency parsing algorithm is a combination of heuristic repair with a complete search of up to two domains of variables in order to ensure that local maxima can be overcome. This algorithm was tested with a manually written grammar on German sentences. A comparison of this approach with a complete search Foth (1999) showed that in 80% of the cases, the same solution is found, in 10% the repair method provides inferior analyses, but for 10% of the sentences, the analyses of the repair methods are better. Half of these cases are sentences for which the complete search could not find any analysis.

5.3 SUMMARY AND FURTHER READING

In this chapter, we looked at grammar-based parsing and related issues. We concentrated on two different approaches to grammar-based parsing: The first approach is based on the finding that projective dependency grammars can be transformed into context-free grammars. This is based on work by Gaifman (1965) and Hays (1964) in the 1960s.

The more efficient Unfold-Fold conversion, which represents each word as two separate items was introduced by Eisner and Blatz (2007) and Johnson (2007). Bilexical probability models in the context of dependency parsing were introduced by Eisner (1996a,b). He suggested bilexical dependency grammars and a CKY-like chart parser that allows for efficient parsing of dependencies. A more thorough investigation of the properties of this algorithm can be found in Eisner (2000). Eisner and Satta (1999) present an efficient parser for parsing bilexical dependency grammars using the split-head representation described in section 5.1.1. Eisner and Smith (2005) extend the probability model of Eisner's parser to include a preference for short-distance dependencies. They show that the modified probability model improves parsing performance in terms of accuracy and time requirements for English and Chinese but not for German.

While Eisner's parsing model is based on bottom-up parsing, there is a parsing model based on link grammar that works top-down (Sleator and Temperley, 1993). Link grammar is very similar to dependency grammar; one of the major differences is that links are not directed. The parser proceeds by setting up a link between two words w_i and w_j based on the linking requirements of w_i and w_j; then it attempts to link all the words between w_i and w_j. Lafferty et al. (1992) describe a probability model for the link grammar parser.

Pro3Gres is another grammar-based dependency parser for English. In Pro3Gres (Schneider, 2004; Schneider et al., 2004), a combination of chunk parsing (Abney, 1991) and CKY parsing is used with a probability model that relies on distances but does not take part-of-speech tags into account.

A good introduction to learning PCFGs can be found in Manning and Schütze (2000). Extensions to PCFGs have also been studied in the context of dependency parsing, most notably the generative statistical parsers of Collins (1999) and Charniak (2000), which have been very influential in constituency-based parsing for English. Collins et al. (1999) applied the Collins parser to the Prague Dependency Treebank of Czech, and Hall and Novák (2005) used both the Collins parser and the Charniak parser to parse Czech, adding a corrective probability model for recovering non-projective dependencies in post-processing. Zeman (2004) and Zeman and Žabokrtský (2005) investigate combining a number of grammar-based models including those based on the Collins and Charniak parsers, as well as others. Another example of a combination of constituent and dependency parsing can be found in the Stanford Parser (Klein and Manning, 2002, 2003), which combines CFG structures and dependency structures in a factored model.

The second approach to grammar-based dependency parsing defines the problem as constraint satisfaction. Here, the grammar consists of constraints. The constraint-based parsing method was introduced by Maruyama (1990). The Hamburg group around Wolfgang Menzel, who implemented a constraint dependency parser (CDG) for German, used the same techniques for their basic system but added weights to the constraints (Menzel and Schröder, 1998; Foth and Menzel, 2005; Schröder et al., 2000). The parser was then extended to perform the transformation-based search with repair (Foth, 1999; Schröder, 2002; Foth et al., 2004, 2005). The German grammar is manually written and consists of approximately 700 constraints. A description of the constraint grammar for German can be found in Foth (2007). Since the manual assignment of weights for so many constraints is difficult, the group also experimented with a machine learning approach based on genetic algorithms (Schröder et al., 2001, 2002). The results show that when starting with the manually assigned weights, the learning method achieves a moderate increase in quality. When starting with randomly assigned weights, the learning approach results in a performance level that is close to the manual results but does not reach them.

The constraint propagation approach was also used in PARSEC (Harper and Helzerman, 1995; Harper et al., 1995), a dependency parser that was developed for integration into a speech recognition system. Harper et al. developed a learning approach for constraint dependency parsing based on *abstract role values* (ARV), which describes a dependency between two words but abstracts over their exact positions. Instead, only a relative position is given. Wang and Harper extend the approach to a probabilistic model using SuperARVs (Wang and Harper, 2002, 2004), which are reminiscent of supertags in tree-adjoining grammar (Bangalore and Joshi, 1999). Parsing with SuperARVs is a two-stage process: In the first step, each word is assigned the best SuperARVs, and in the second step, the dependency requirements of the SuperARVs are resolved. This is similar to Eisner's probability model B (Eisner, 1996a).

Constraint propagation is central also to Topological Dependency Grammar (Duchier, 1999; Duchier and Debusmann, 2001), which divides the set of grammatical constraints into immediate dominance (ID) and linear precedence constraints (LP) in a way which is reminiscent of work on ID/LP-grammars for constituency-based representations. The most recent development of this framework is called Extensible Dependency Grammar, where the division is generalized to arbitrarily many dimensions, including also dimensions of semantics and information structure (Debusmann et al., 2004).

Lin's MINIPAR (Lin, 1998a) is a principle-based parser that encodes grammatical principles from the theory of Government and Binding (Chomsky, 1981) as weighted constraints. Parsing is performed with distributed charts, that is, each word maintains a chart with partial results pertaining to the grammatical category of the word. In order to coordinate parsing between different words, MINIPAR employs a message passing algorithm.

CHAPTER 6

Evaluation

In this chapter, we will consider the practical side of dependency parsing. First, we will discuss different evaluation metrics. Then we will discuss a suggestion for using dependency representations to compare parsers based on different grammar formalisms, and we will discuss how constituent treebanks can be converted into a dependency representation. This is an important conversion since for many languages, only constituent-based treebanks are available. We will also have a quick look at the shared tasks on dependency parsing of the Conference on Computational Natural Language Learning (CoNLL) because they provide many valuable resources.

6.1 EVALUATION METRICS

The standard methodology for evaluating dependency parsers, as well as other kinds of parsers, is to apply them to a test set taken from a treebank and compare the output of the parser to the gold standard annotation found in the treebank. Dependency parsing has been evaluated with many different evaluation metrics. The most widely used metrics are listed here:

- **Exact match:** This is the percentage of completely correctly parsed sentences. The same measure is also used for the evaluation of constituent parsers.

- **Attachment score:** This is the percentage of words that have the correct head. The use of a single accuracy metric is possible in dependency parsing thanks to the single-head property of dependency trees, which makes parsing resemble a tagging task, where every word is to be tagged with its correct head and dependency type. This is unlike the standard metrics in constituency-based parsing, which are based on precision and recall, since it is not possible to assume a one-to-one correspondence between constituents in the parser output and constituents in the treebank annotation.

- **Precision/Recall:** If we relax the single-head property or if we want to evaluate single dependency types, the following metrics can be used. They correspond more directly to the metrics used for constituent parsing.

  - **Precision:** This is the percentage of dependencies with a specific type in the parser output that were correct.

  - **Recall:** This is the percentage of dependencies with a specific type in the test set that were correctly parsed.

  - $\mathbf{F}_{\beta=1}$ **measure:** This is the harmonic mean of precision and recall.

All of these metrics can be unlabeled (only looking at heads) or labeled (looking at heads and labels). The most commonly used metrics are the *labeled attachment score* (LAS) and the *unlabeled attachment score* (UAS).

LAS, as we have presented it above, gives an evaluation of how many words were parsed correctly. However, this may not always be the point of interest. Another way of evaluating the quality of dependency parses is using sentences as the basic units. In this case, we calculate for each sentence what the percentage of correct dependencies is and then average over the sentences. The difference becomes clear when we look at a test set containing 2 sentences: Let us assume that for the first sentence, the parser assigned correct dependencies to 9 out of 10 words. For the second sentence, we have 15 out 45 words correct. The word-based LAS would be $LAS_w = (9 + 15)/(10 + 45) = 0.436$. The sentence-based LAS is calculated as $LAS_s = (9/10 + 15/45)/2 = (0.9 + 0.333)/2 = 0.617$.

In the light of this distinction, we can call the word-based LAS *micro-average* LAS and the sentence-based one a *macro-average* LAS. Another way of calculating a macro-average LAS is by averaging over all dependency types.

6.2 DEPENDENCIES FOR CROSS-FRAMEWORK PARSER EVALUATION

With the advent of many broad coverage (constituent) parsers, the problem of comparing the different analyses of these parsers became obvious. It is very difficult to compare parsers that produce deep trees with parsers that produce flatter trees. One possibility would be to perform task-based (in vivo) evaluation, i.e., evaluation in a system that uses a parser as a component, such as a machine translation system or a question answering system. By integrating different parsers, we can compare the system's performance given a specific parser. This is normally not done because of the lack of systems that can easily integrate different parsers without adaptation.

An additional problem for in vitro evaluation is that the standard evaluation metrics for constituent parsing, *precision* and *recall*, evaluate one attachment error as causing errors on all levels whose spans are affected by the attachment. This can be shown with the following example adapted from Lin (1995):

[[Bellows [made [the request]]] [while [[the all-woman jury] [was [out [of [the courtroom]]]]]]]
[Bellows [[made [the request]] [while [[the [[all-woman] jury]] [was [out [of [the courtroom]]]]]]]]

One of the differences between the two analyses is that in the first case, the *while* clause is the sister of the first clause while in the second analysis, it is a sister of the verb phrase *made the request*. An evaluation of these trees results in a recall of 81.8% and in a precision of 75.0%, which seems excessive for a single attachment error.

A possible way of leveling the differences between flat and deep trees, as well as the high error counts resulting from different attachment levels, is first converting both the original treebank tree and the parser output into dependencies and then evaluating on the latter. The dependency format has the advantage that all structures are reduced to one dependency relation per word, thus equalizing the differences between different parsers. However, if the output of different parsers using different grammars needs to be compared, the conversion to a single dependency format with a predefined label set will result in cases in which information is lost. This problem occurs when the parser makes more fine-grained distinctions than the dependency grammar. The other case, in which the dependency grammar makes more fine-grained distinctions than the parser, is even more difficult. In this case, the conversion would need to employ heuristics to determine which dependency label to use in any given case. This results in errors introduced by the conversion process. Crouch et al. (2002) report an error of 2 percentage points in a case where they converted the output of an LFG-based parser into a dependency representation. One possibility to at least partially avoid these problems is the use of a hierarchy of categories so that the evaluation can be performed on a fine-grained level as well as on coarser-grained levels. For example, such a hierarchy might specify a rather generic term *argument*, which can be either a *subject* or a *complement*. Complements can then be split further into *phrasal object* and *clausal complement*. If a parser does not distinguish between different types of complements, it can still be evaluated on the coarser level of *complement*.

6.3 CONVERTING CONSTITUENT TREEBANKS INTO DEPENDENCY FORMATS

So far, we have presupposed the existence of a dependency grammar or a treebank in dependency format. Many treebanks, however, are annotated with constituent structure. The standard treebank for English, the Penn Treebank (Marcus et al., 1993), is an example of such a constituent-based treebank. If we start from such a treebank, we need to convert the treebank to a dependency format if we wish to build a dependency parser over the resource. In cases where the constituent analysis is augmented by grammatical functions (such as *subject, object, head, non-head*), the conversion is straightforward: For each constituent, we determine its head. All the other words and constituents are treated as dependents of the head, and their grammatical function can be used as the label for the dependency. For the constituent structure in the upper half of figure 6.1, for example, we can see that the verb phrase (VP) is the head of the S constituent, *would* is the head of the VP, and *I* is the head of the subject noun phrase (NP). From this information, we can deduce that there is a dependency *would* → *I*. The whole dependency graph is shown in the lower half of figure 6.1.

In most constituency-annotated treebanks, however, only certain grammatical functions are annotated explicitly. Head/non-head information is generally implicitly encoded, for example when an X-bar scheme underlies the annotation. In such cases, the conversion needs to be based on head finding heuristics. Such rules specify, for each constituent type, which daughter nodes can serve as heads, in which order they should be searched, and from which direction in the constituent. An example for such a head-finding heuristic for prepositional phrases (PP) is given below.

PP   right   IN TO VBG VBN RP FW

```
( (S
   (NP-SBJ I/PRP-HD )
   (VP-HD would/MD-HD
    (VP like/VB-HD
      (S
         (NP-SBJ it/PRP )
         (VP-HD to/TO
           (VP-HD have/VB-HD
             (NP
               (NP-HD a/DT stop/NN-HD )
               (PP-LOC in/IN-HD
                 (NP Boston/NNP-HD )))))))))
```

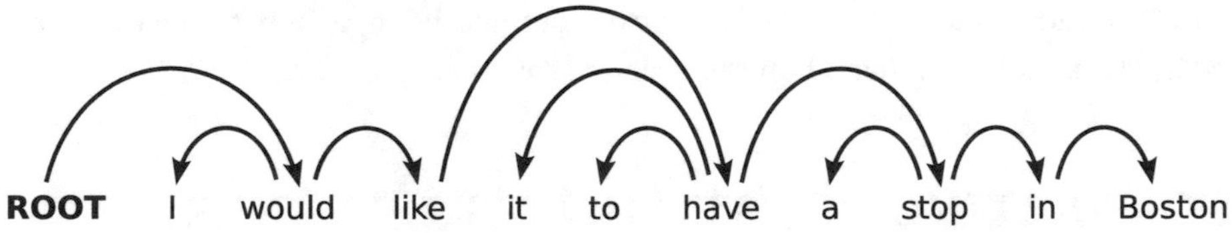

Figure 6.1: CFG tree with head information and its dependency representation.

This heuristic states that we search from left to right among the constituents of the PP. If we find a preposition (IN), we have the head; if the phrase does not contain a preposition, we next look for a word with the part-of-speech tag TO, and so forth.

Since the constituent tree often does not contain grammatical functions, the dependencies are either unlabeled or labeled with a combination of the involved constituents. Thus, the dependency between *would* and *I* could be labeled SBJ since the NP is marked as the subject. If this were not the case, we could label this dependency with the label NP_S_VP stating that the mother node of the partial tree is the S node, the left constituent is an NP, and the right constituent a VP. This helps to distinguish subject NPs from objects (which are not attached at the S level). Such dependency annotations can be used with any dependency parsing algorithms discussed in this book as well as with head-driven statistical parsers such as the one by Collins (1999).

6.4   THE CoNLL SHARED TASKS ON DEPENDENCY PARSING

The Conference on Computational Natural Language Learning (CoNLL) features a shared task each year, in which participants train and test their learning systems on exactly the same data sets, in order to compare systems under the same conditions. Apart from the results of the systems that are published at the conferences, the shared tasks have also resulted in very useful repositories for standardized data sets, overviews of systems, and evaluation software. In 2006 and 2007, the shared task was devoted to dependency parsing. In 2006, the focus was on multilingual dependency parsing. In 2007, there were two separate tracks: one track continued the theme of multilingual dependency parsing, and the other track was concerned with domain adaptation. In 2008, the shared task was an extension of the previous tasks: joint learning of syntactic and semantic dependencies. All three shared tasks produced very informative web pages: `http://nextens.uvt.nl/~conll/` for 2006, `http://nextens.uvt.nl/depparse-wiki/SharedTaskWebsite` for 2007, and `http://www.yr-bcn.es/conll2008/` for 2008.

One of the most important outcomes of the 2006 shared task was the data format, a slight modification of which is in the process of becoming a standard for dependency parsing. The data format is an 8 column format,[1] based on the Malt-TAB format (cf. `http://w3.msi.vxu.se/~nivre/research/MaltXML.html`). The 8 columns are:

1. **ID**: Word counter, starts at 1 for each sentence.

2. **FORM**: Word form or punctuation symbol.

3. **LEMMA**: Lemma or stem if available.

4. **CPOSTAG**: Coarse-grained part-of-speech tag.

5. **POSTAG**: Fine-grained part-of-speech tag. If only one part-of-speech tagset is available, this column has the same value as the previous one.

6. **FEATS**: Unordered set of syntactic and/or morphological features if available. Individual features are separated by a vertical bar.

7. **HEAD**: Head of the current word. This is either the ID value of another token or 0 if the word depends on the virtual root of the sentence (ROOT).

8. **DEPREL**: The dependency relation (label) to the head. If HEAD=0, the dependency relation may either be a meaningful label or have the default value ROOT.

Columns 1 through 6 represent possible types of information that are given as input to the parser. If values are unavailable, the columns contain underscores. Columns 7 and 8 contain the information to be learned. Figure 6.2 shows a dependency graph for a Dutch sentence and its representation in the CoNLL dependency format.

The shared task 2006 featured 13 languages from 7 language families: Arabic, Chinese, Czech, Danish, Dutch, German, Japanese, Portuguese, Slovene, Spanish, Swedish, Turkish, and optionally Bulgarian. The training sets ranged from 1 500 (Arabic, Slovene) to 72 000 sentences (Czech). The test sets were selected so that they contained approximately 5 000 words.

The multilingual track of the shared task 2007 featured 10 languages from 9 language families: Arabic, Basque, Catalan, Chinese, Czech, English, Greek, Hungarian, Italian, and Turkish. For the

---

[1]The original format contains 2 more columns, which are almost never used, so we refrain from presenting them here.

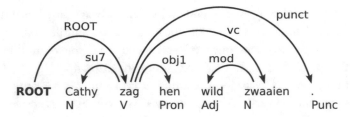

1	Cathy	Cathy	N	N	eigen|ev|neut	2	su7
2	zag	zie	V	V	trans|ovt|1of2of3|ev	0	ROOT
3	hen	hen	Pron	Pron	per|3|mv|datofacc	2	obj1
4	wild	wild	Adj	Adj	attr|stell|onverv	5	mod
5	zwaaien	zwaai	N	N	soort|mv|neut	2	vc
6	.	.	Punc	Punc	punt	5	punct

Figure 6.2: Dependency graph and its representation in the CoNLL column format.

training sets, an upper limit of 500 000 words was introduced, which led to a reduced training set for Czech as compared to the 2006 Czech training set. As a consequence, the training sets varied between 2 700 (Greek) and 25 400 (Czech) sentences. The target size for test sets was again set to 5 000 words.

The domain adaptation track 2007 used English as the only language. The training data consisted of a dependency version of the Penn treebank (Marcus et al., 1993), which was also used as training data for English in the multilingual track. The participants were provided with a small development set from the biochemical domain as well as with large sets of unlabeled data from all domains (training, development, and test). The data for the tests came from two different domains: chemical abstracts (Kulick et al., 2004) and parent-child dialogs from the CHILDES corpus (MacWhinney, 2000).

All the data sets are still available although most of them require licenses. More information can be found on the web sites.

In 2006, 19 systems participated. In 2007, 23 systems participated in the multilingual track and 10 systems in the domain adaptation track. For reasons of space, we will not discuss the domain adaptation track further, but will concentrate on the top scores reached for the languages in 2006 and 2007. Complete lists of results can be found on the web pages and in the overview papers (Buchholz and Marsi, 2006; Nivre, Hall, Kübler, McDonald, Nilsson, Riedel and Yuret, 2007). The results for 2006 are shown in table 6.1, the results for the multilingual track in 2007 in table 6.2.

The results show that dependency parsing can be successfully applied to a wide variety of languages. However, there are differences in performance for different languages, with the labeled attachment score ranging from 91.65% for Japanese to 65.68% for Turkish and 66.91% for Arabic

Table 6.1: Top scoring results for the 13 languages in the CoNLL 2006 shared task. Ar=Arabic, Ch=Chinese, Cz=Czech, Da=Danish, Du=Dutch, Ge=German, Ja=Japanese, Po=Portuguese, Sl=Slovene, Sp=Spanish, Sw=Swedish, Tu=Turkish, Bu=Bulgarian.

Language	Ar	Ch	Cz	Da	Du	Ge	Ja	Po	Sl
LAS	66.91	89.96	80.18	84.79	79.19	87.34	91.65	87.60	73.44
UAS	79.39	93.18	97.30	90.58	83.57	90.38	93.16	91.36	83.17

Language	Sp	Sw	Tu	Bu
LAS	82.25	84.58	65.68	87.57
UAS	86.05	89.54	75.82	91.72

Table 6.2: Top scoring results for the 10 languages in the CoNLL 2007 shared task (multilingual track). Ar=Arabic, Ba=Basque, Ca=Catalan, Ch=Chinese, Cz=Czech, En=English, Gr=Greek, Hu=Hungarian, It=Italian, Tu=Turkish.

Language	Ar	Ba	Ca	Ch	Cz	En	Gr	Hu
LAS	76.52	76.94	88.70	84.69	80.19	89.61	76.31	80.27
UAS	86.09	82.84	93.40	88.94	86.28	90.63	84.08	83.55

Language	It	Tu
LAS	84.40	79.81
UAS	87.91	86.22

(in 2006). However, note that the two languages which proved to be the most difficult ones in 2006, Turkish and Arabic, were also used in 2007. The best results in 2007 for these languages were considerably better (79.81% LAS for Turkish[2] and 67.52% for Arabic). In the 2007 multilingual track, the languages can be separated into three classes with respect to top scores:

- Low (76.31–76.94):
  Arabic, Basque, Greek

- Medium (79.81–80.27):
  Czech, Hungarian, Turkish

- High (84.40–89.61):
  Catalan, Chinese, English, Italian

It is interesting to see that the classes are more easily definable via language characteristics than via characteristics of the data sets. The split goes across training set size, original data format (constituent vs. dependency), sentence length, percentage of unknown words, number of dependency

---

[2]However, it should be pointed out that the rules for scoring intra-word dependencies in Turkish changed from 2006 and 2007, so that the net gain in accuracy was 7–8 percentage points, rather than 14.

labels, and ratio of part-of-speech tags and dependency labels. The class with the highest top scores contains languages with a rather impoverished morphology. Medium scores were reached by the two agglutinative languages, Hungarian and Turkish, as well as by Czech. The most difficult languages were those that combine a relatively free word order with a high degree of inflection. Based on these characteristics, one would expect to find Czech in the last class. However, the Czech training set is four times the size of the training set for Arabic, which is the language with the largest training set of the difficult languages. In the 2006 set, there are no clear classes with respect to top scores. Some languages, such as Turkish, fit into the 2007 pattern, and for Japanese, the high results can be explained by its genre, dialogs. However, there is no overall pattern, and the results cannot easily be explained by data set or language characteristics.

6.5   SUMMARY AND FURTHER READING

This chapter started out by giving an overview of the evaluation metrics used for dependency parsing. After looking at a method for using dependency representations to evaluate parsers based on different linguistic frameworks, we discussed how constituent treebanks can be converted into dependency representations. Finally, we gave an overview of the CoNLL shared tasks on dependency parsing. The discussion of shared tasks leads to the question of how to compare the different dependency parsing algorithms presented in this book, which we look at in chapter 7.

For many languages, there exists a constituent-based but no dependency-based treebank. In general, it is possible to convert such treebanks into dependencies. The resulting representation can be used for stand-alone dependency parsing as well as for CFG parsing augmented with dependencies. To our knowledge, the first such conversion was used by Magerman (1995). There are many different head finding tables for the Penn treebank all ultimately based on Magerman's original heuristics. One of the better documented versions can be found in Collins (1999). A description of the conversion algorithm can be found in Lin (1998b). A converter from the Penn Treebank format to dependencies was developed by Johansson and Nugues (2007a). This converter was used for the CoNLL shared tasks 2006 and 2007. The hierarchy of dependencies was suggested by Carroll et al. (1998). A whole range of suggestions for new evaluation metrics, many of which center around using dependency representations in one form or another, can be found in Carroll (2002). Overviews of the CoNLL shared tasks were presented by Buchholz and Marsi (2006) for 2006, by Nivre, Hall, Kübler, McDonald, Nilsson, Riedel and Yuret (2007) for 2007, and by Surdeanu et al. (2008) for 2008.

CHAPTER 7

Comparison

In previous chapters, we have discussed a few of the more prominent approaches to dependency parsing that are in use today. We have attempted to make connections between each approach in the text of these chapters, but this was often in passing and without the treatment that the topic deserves. In this chapter, we aim to contrast different approaches both theoretically and empirically when possible. We start by looking at the two purely data-driven methods examined in this book: transition-based and graph-based parsing. We look at how these methods are different theoretically and how these differences manifest themselves in empirical parsing accuracy. We then shift our focus to comparing data-driven and grammar-based approaches and attempt to draw connections between model assumptions and the resulting algorithms for producing dependency trees.

7.1 COMPARING TRANSITION-BASED AND GRAPH-BASED MODELS

Before we dive into the comparison, it is worth summarizing quickly both transition-based and graph-based parsing in terms of parameterization and parsing algorithms.

- **Parameterization:** Transition-based systems parameterize models over transitions in an abstract state machine, where each state (or configuration) represents a dependency graph. This allows these models to create rich feature representations over possible next transitions as well as all previous transitions that have occurred to bring the system into the current state. Conversely, graph-based models parameterize over subgraphs of the resulting dependency tree. As such, these models have a rather impoverished feature representation with a very local scope – often just over a single arc – and cannot model decisions on a truly global scale.

- **Parsing Algorithms:** Transition-based models use greedy algorithms to move from one configuration to the next by simply choosing the most likely next transition. Such a greedy approach cannot provide any guarantees that mistakes made early in the process do not propagate to decisions at later stages – a defect often called *error propagation*. On the other hand, graph-based models can often search the space of dependency trees, with guarantees that the returned dependency tree is the most likely under the model parameters. This is true for arc-factored models as well as many projective non-arc-factored models.

These differences highlight an inherent trade-off between exact parsing algorithms and the expressiveness of feature representations. Graph-based models favor the former at the expense of the latter and transition-based models the opposite. This trade-off is not artificial. Increasing parameterization for graph-based systems results in a loss of parsing efficiency. Furthermore, there is no natural

Table 7.1: Labeled parsing accuracy for top scoring graph and transition-based systems at CoNLL 2006.

Language	Ar	Bu	Ch	Cz	Da	Du	Ge	Ja
Transition-based	66.71	87.41	86.92	78.42	84.77	78.59	85.82	91.65
Graph-based	66.91	87.57	85.90	80.18	84.79	79.19	87.34	90.71

Language	Po	Sl	Sp	Sw	Tu	Average
Transition-based	87.60	70.30	81.29	84.58	65.68	80.75
Graph-based	86.82	73.44	82.25	82.55	63.19	80.83

notion of globally optimal search in transition-based parsers. Even if such a notion could be precisely defined, it most likely would require limiting the possible features in order for efficient algorithms to be defined. This naturally raises a question: Does this trade-off in data-driven models manifest itself empirically?

The study of McDonald and Nivre (2007) attempt to answer this question and we summarize their main findings here. McDonald and Nivre conducted a detailed empirical comparison in the performance of a transition-based parser and a graph-based parser on the CoNLL 2006 data set. As described in the previous chapter, this data set consisted of 13 different languages. The two highest-scoring systems on these data sets were one transition-based and one graph-based model, whose LAS scores can be seen in table 7.1. At first glance, this analysis suggests that there is not much difference between the two models. There is some variability between languages, but on average, the systems have remarkably similar accuracies with only an absolute difference of 0.08%. However, a closer look at the kinds of errors each system makes reveals that average LAS is misleading.

To see this, one can look at both structural properties of dependency trees and linguistic properties of the input (in the form of surface syntax) or output (in the form of dependency relations). Structural properties measure LAS for arcs relative to different contexts in the tree, which can include: *root-distance*, which is the distance of an arc from the root; *arc-length*, which is the number of words between the head and the dependent in the sentence; *neighborhood-size*, which is the number of arcs in the same horizontal neighborhood (i.e., among words that share the same head); *arc-degree*, which is the degree of non-projectivity of the arc (Nivre, 2006a); etc. When looking at micro-averages relative to these properties, interesting patterns begin to emerge. In particular, transition-based parsers are more accurate than graph-based models for arcs that are further away from the root and have a smaller arc-length. When examining the fundamental trade-off between exact parsing algorithms and rich feature representations, this distinction seems to make sense. Since transition-based systems suffer from potential error propagation, we can expect lower accuracies for decisions made later in the search, such as those nearer to the root and with longer arc lengths. This is precisely what happens, and there is a marked degradation of accuracy as distance to the root shortens or dependency length lengthens. On the other hand, there is no theoretical reason that graph-based systems should be more accurate for any type of arc property since the search is exact.[1] This is manifested in more uniform accuracies relative to tree properties.

Relating model accuracy to a set of linguistic properties, such as parts of speech (relative to the dependent in the arc) and dependency types, also reveals interesting properties. Given the important typological differences that exist between languages, as well as the diversity of annotation schemes used in different treebanks, it is far from straight-forward to compare these categories across languages. Nevertheless, McDonald and Nivre identify a few broad categories that are cross-linguistically consistent. For parts of speech, this includes *verbs* (including both main verbs and auxiliaries), *nouns* (including proper names), *pronouns* (sometimes also including determiners), *adjectives*, *adverbs*, *adpositions* (prepositions, postpositions), and *conjunctions* (both coordinating and subordinating). For dependency relation types, this includes a general *root* category (for labels used on arcs from the artificial root, including either a generic label or the label assigned to predicates of main clauses, which are normally verbs), a *subject* category, and an *object* category (including both direct and indirect objects). Unfortunately, many interesting types could not be identified with high enough precision across languages, such as adverbials, which cannot be clearly distinguished in annotation schemes that subsume them under a general modifier category, and coordinate structures, which are sometimes annotated with special dependency types, and sometimes with ordinary dependency types found also in non-coordinated structures.

If one examines the errors at the part-of-speech level, it is seen that transition-based methods tend to have better accuracy for nouns and pronouns, while graph-based methods are better on all other categories, in particular verbs and conjunctions. This pattern is consistent with the analysis of structural properties insofar as verbs and conjunctions are often involved in dependencies closer to the root and with longer arc distances, while nouns and pronouns are typically attached to verbs and therefore occur lower in the tree and with shorter arc distances. Looking at the data, average distance to the root is 3.1 for verbs and 3.8 for conjunctions, but 4.7 for nouns and 4.9 for pronouns; the average dependency length is 4.2 for verbs, 4.8 for conjunctions, 2.3 for nouns, and 1.6 for pronouns. Adverbs resemble verbs and conjunctions with respect to root distance (3.7) but group with nouns and pronouns for dependency length (2.3). Adpositions and especially adjectives are the only parts of speech that appear to break this pattern. With a root distance of 4.4/5.2 and an arc length of 2.5/1.5, we would expect transition-based models to be much more accurate when, in fact, they are not.

Finally, when one considers precision and recall for dependents of the root node (mostly verbal predicates) and for subjects and objects, similar patterns emerge. Graph-based models have considerably better precision (and slightly better recall) for the root category, but transition-based models have an advantage for the nominal categories, especially subjects. A possible explanation for the latter result, in addition to the graph-based factors invoked before, is that transition-based models may use previously assigned dependency labels as features (due to their ability to incorporate

---

[1]Technically, for the particular graph-based instantiation used in the experiments of McDonald and Nivre (2007), which is the system of McDonald et al. (2006), the search is exact relative to projective trees with an approximate post-processing step to introduce non-projective arcs.

rich feature representations over past decisions). This may sometimes be important to disambiguate subjects and objects in particular for free word order languages where these dependencies may not have a fixed ordering relative to the verb.

The McDonald and Nivre study highlights the fundamental trade-off between transition-based and graph-based models, where the former prefers rich feature representations at the cost of sub-optimal parsing algorithms, and graph-based methods the opposite, and shows that this trade-off does manifest itself empirically. Error propagation is an issue for transition-based systems, which typically perform worse on long distance arcs and arcs higher in the tree. But this is offset by the rich feature representation available to these models that result in better decisions for frequently occurring classes of arcs like short dependencies or subject and object dependents. The errors for graph-based models are spread a little more evenly as one might expect due to the fact that inference algorithms and feature representations should not theoretically perform better for one type of arc than another.

The fact the transition-based and graph-based parsers make markedly different mistakes suggests that there might be empirical gains by combining the two types of parsers. Recently, there has been much positive evidence suggesting that even simple methods for combining transition-based and graph-based parser yields significant improvements across all languages. These methods usually take one of two forms. In the first, many variations of graph and transition-based parsers are created and a meta-system uses the outputs of each in a majority voting scheme to select a single parse. Voting, in such systems, can be either over entire trees or over individual arcs. The second method that is common is to use the output of one parser, say a transition-based parser, as additional input to the other parser, in this case a graph-based parser. Such methods are referred to as *stacked classifiers* or *stacked parsers*. These achieve superior performance by allowing the second parser to learn relative to the first parser's strengths and weaknesses, which allows the second parser to use the predictions of the first parser when advantageous and ignore them when not.

7.2   COMPARING GRAMMAR-BASED AND DATA-DRIVEN MODELS

The close connection between context-free dependency grammars and projective graph-based dependency parsing has been touched upon throughout both chapters 3 and 4. These systems share parsing algorithms (CKY and Eisner's algorithm) and can even share probability models (e.g., bilexical generative models). Perhaps the simplest way of stating this relationship is to say that projective graph-based models are in fact just context-free dependency grammars where the underlying grammar generates all possible strings, i.e., the language generated by the grammar Γ is $L = \Sigma^*$, and all possible trees, i.e., $\mathcal{G}_S$ for all $S \in \Sigma^*$. Of course, the advantage of graph-based systems comes from assuming a weaker underlying formalism, which results in the ability to exploit graph-theoretic algorithms to search efficiently for non-projective trees.

However, even when we allow for non-projectivity, there is still a connection between graph-based and grammar-based models. In particular, if one constrains the structure of dependency trees so that they are well-nested, which measures the level of overlap between distinct subtrees of the tree, and have a gap-degree of at most 1, which measures the discontinuity in the yield of nodes in the tree, then it can be shown that this class of trees corresponds directly to LTAG derivations (Bodirsky et al., 2005). Again, if we consider a graph-based method as simply an LTAG that generates the language Σ^*, then a simple connection with LTAG can be established in the non-projective case. This raises the question: Is it possible to constrain the Chu-Liu-Edmonds algorithms to parse dependency trees that are well-nested and have a bounded gap-degree, all in polynomial time? Probably not, as the complexity of LTAG is well studied and lower-bounds are far in excess of the $O(n^2)$ run-time of Chu-Liu-Edmonds. As a result, any graph-based parsing algorithm that constrains well-nestedness or gap-degree is most likely to take the form of LTAG algorithms, which themselves are based on chart-parsing techniques (just like CKY and Eisner's algorithm) and not greedy-recursive techniques (like the Chu-Liu-Edmonds algorithm).

Projective transition-based parsing algorithms also have a strong connection to a context-free counterpart. If one applies the same transformations from dependency trees to context-free phrase structure as presented in section 5.1, then it is possible to use transition-based parsing algorithms to parse a context-free grammar. This is because similar transition algorithms can be defined for phrase structure, which are commonly called shift-reduce parsing algorithms in that body of literature (Briscoe and Carroll, 1993). Just as in the case of dependencies, these shift-reduce parsing algorithms can be shown to be sound and complete, but instead with respect to context-free phrase structure. Thus, it is possible to first convert a set of dependency trees to phrase-structure, train a shift-reduce parsing model and use it to parse new sentences and reconstruct the dependency trees from the resulting output. Again, these transition-based models correspond to their grammar-based equivalents under the assumption that the grammar generates the language Σ^*.

Although less direct, there are also many strong connections between constraint dependency grammars and purely data-driven models, most notably graph-based systems. These connections are most apparent when we consider the parsing algorithms employed by both types of models. In constraint-based parsing, all models begin by considering the complete dependency graph for a sentence (previously called G_S) and attempt to satisfy a set of weighted constraints. In the same vein, graph-based models start with the complete graph and then attempt to satisfy a set of constraints (i.e., the root, single-head and acyclicity properties of dependency trees). Though constraints are not weighted directly in graph-based parsing, there is a weighting on arcs that must be maximized while satisfying the constraints. In fact, we can be explicit about this view of graph-based parsing by formulating it as an Integer Linear Programming (ILP) problem, which consists of optimizing a linear objective relative to a set of linear constraints. Consider an input sentence S with the goal of producing a dependency tree $G = (V, A) \in \mathcal{G}_S$. First, let us define a set of variables:

- $a_{ij}^r \in \{0, 1\}$, where $a_{ij}^r = 1$ if and only if $(w_i, r, w_j) \in A$

- $\mathbf{a}$ is the vector of all variables a_{ij}^r

Now, let's consider the following ILP:

$$\underset{\mathbf{a}}{\operatorname{argmax}} \sum_{i,j,r} a_{ij}^r \times \lambda_{(w_i, r, w_j)}$$

such that:
$$\sum_{i,r} a_{i0}^r = 0 \qquad \text{(unique root)}$$
$$\text{for all } j > 0, \ \sum_{i,r} a_{ij}^r = 1 \qquad \text{(single head)}$$
$$\text{for all possible cycles } C, \ \sum_{(w_i, r, w_j) \in C} a_{ij}^r \leq |C| - 1 \qquad \text{(acyclic)}$$

This ILP problem can be solved with a variety of techniques and we can take the resulting vector $\mathbf{a}$ and construct the tree $G = (V, A)$ by setting $A = \{(w_i, r, w_j) \mid a_{ij}^r = 1 \text{ in } \mathbf{a}\}$. The constraints enforce that the assignments of values to $\mathbf{a}$ result in a dependency tree rooted out of w_0 as they ensure that the graph is spanning, acyclic and that each non-root has exactly one head in the tree.

There are two drawbacks with this approach. First, ILP problems are in general intractable, whereas it is known that we can already solve this problem using the Chu-Liu-Edmonds algorithm, which has a polynomial run-time. However, ILPs are well-studied optimization problems that can often be solved efficiently using cutting-plane, branch-and-bound or other common algorithmic techniques. The second problem is that the set of constraints in the above optimization is exponential in the size of the input. This is due to the third constraint enumerating all possible cycles. It is possible to combat this by introducing an auxiliary variable:

- $b_{ij} \in \{0, 1\}$ where $b_{ij} = 1$ if there is a directed path from $w_i \rightarrow^* w_j$ in G

Note that the definition of b_{ij} does not state that when $b_{ij} = 1$ there must be such a path in G, but only that if there is such a path then $b_{ij} = 1$. The weaker definition is sufficient for our purposes and makes the resulting optimization simpler. Using this new auxiliary variable, we can then replace the acyclicity constraint by the following three constraints:

$$\text{for all } i, j, r, b_{ij} - a_{ij}^r \geq 0$$
$$\text{for all } i, j, k, b_{ik} - b_{ij} - b_{jk} \geq -1$$
$$\text{for all } i \geq 0, b_{ii} = 0$$

The first two constraints serve to ensure that assignments to b_{ij} satisfy its definition and the third constraint forces the returned graph to be acyclic. The first constraint ties the variables a_{ij}^r and b_{ij} together by stating that if there is an arc from w_i to w_j with any label, then there must be a path of length one from word w_i to w_j represented in b. The second constraint enforces the transitive closure of the directed path relationship encoded by b_{ij} and thus covers all those paths of length greater than 1. It does this by ensuring that if $w_i \rightarrow^* w_j$ ($b_{ij} = 1$) and $w_j \rightarrow^* w_k$ ($b_{jk} = 1$) then $w_i \rightarrow^* w_k$ ($b_{ik} = 1$). Thus, from all length one paths we get all length two paths, and from all length one and length two paths, we get all length three paths, etc. Having ensured that b_{ij} is properly encoded with respect to $\mathbf{a}$, it is trivial to discard cycles. By the definition of b_{ij}, if there were a cycle $w_i \rightarrow^* w_i$ induced by $\mathbf{a}$, then $b_{ii} = 1$. By forcing $b_{ii} = 0$, we eliminate all such assignments and the returned graph must be acyclic.

The optimization was presented here simply to illustrate the close connection between graph-based systems and constraint dependency grammars. By modeling graph-based parsing in such a way, we can begin to incorporate constraints such as "a verb can only have at most one subject":

$$\text{for all } w_i \text{ that are verbs: } \sum_j a_{ij}^{r=\text{SBJ}} \leq 1$$

The graph-based model, in a sense, becomes grammar-based through such linguistic constraints, which are similar to the kinds of constraints a constraint dependency grammar might encode.

In terms of algorithmic form, there are also close connections between the transformation-based parsing algorithms with repair (section 5.2.2) used in constraint dependency grammars and the parsing algorithms used in data-driven systems. Repair algorithms typically start with a high likelihood dependency tree (usually by satisfying some simple unary constraints) and then iteratively attempt to satisfy non-local constraints and move towards an optimal dependency tree. This kind of post-processing is similar to pseudo-projective parsing, where the system starts by returning the most likely projective parse and then transforms the parse through encoded arc labels (section 3.5). The difference is that in constraint dependency grammars, the post-process search is done with respect to the ultimate objective function, whereas in pseudo-projective parsing, the search is done with respect to arc labels that have been encoded before the model is even trained. Perhaps a closer analogy is to search algorithms for non-projective graph-based systems when the model is not arc-factored, in which case parsing is typically NP-hard (see section 4.4). In this case, a common technique is to begin by finding the highest scoring projective tree (which can be done efficiently) and then incrementally making minor adjustments to the tree to introduce non-projectivity if these adjustments increase the overall score. Just as in the case of constraint dependency grammar, this method is approximate and will find a local optimum in the search space, but search is still with respect to the ultimate objective function.

7.3   SUMMARY AND FURTHER READING

In this section, we compared the various dependency parsing systems that were discussed earlier in the book. In particular, we looked at an empirical evaluation of transition-based and graph-based parsing and argued that errors made by each system can be connected to theoretical expectations. This was based primarily on the work of McDonald and Nivre (2007) who give a much more detailed account. Studies on combining graph-based and transition-based parsers can be found in Sagae and Lavie (2006), Martins et al. (2008), Nivre and McDonald (2008), and Zhang and Clark (2008). We then looked at the connections between grammar-based and purely data-driven systems. When context-free (or projective) assumptions are made, then these models are closely related and even equivalent under certain assumptions. There is also a strong connection between constraint dependency grammars and graph-based systems, which can be illustrated by formulating graph-based parsing as an ILP problem. Riedel and Clarke (2006) study graph-based parsing using an ILP formulation both algorithmically and empirically. Transformation-based parsing algorithms with repair used in constraint dependency grammars also have analogs in data-driven systems (Foth, 1999; Schröder, 2002; Foth et al., 2004, 2005). For transition-based models, this can come in the form of pseudo-projective parsing (Nivre and Nilsson, 2005), since both use post-processing techniques over an initial highly likely tree to produce the final tree returned by the system. For graph-based methods, approximate post-process searching starting from a base projective parser also has a similar flavor cf. McDonald and Pereira (2006).

CHAPTER 8

Final Thoughts

Our aim in this book was to provide an in-depth account of the current practices and trends in dependency parsing. We saw these as data-driven parsers, which includes transition-based and graph-based parsing, grammar-based parsers, which includes context-free and constraint-based formalisms, and large-scale multi-lingual parser evaluation. We complemented this with an account of the commonalities and differences between each kind of parser in terms of their algorithmic make-up, theoretical properties, and empirical performance when appropriate studies were available. The approaches covered within these pages certainly does not represent the entire spectrum of research on dependency parsing, but we hope that the further reading sections provided in each chapter as well as the appendix of resources and the extensive bibliography that follow will fill out the remaining gaps. Furthermore, this is a burgeoning research area with a number of new studies being published every year. We have attempted to incorporate the latest in the field, but the reader is of course encouraged to check the latest conference proceedings and journal issues to stay abreast of the developments.

We would like to take these final pages to speculate on what the future of research in dependency parsing might hold. If recent trends are any indication, work on data-driven models will continue to be a major focus. This includes both the application of new learning techniques and the development of new formulations that cannot be characterized as either transition-based or graph-based. Further studies at understanding the empirical difference between transition-based and graph-based systems will hopefully lead to additional empirical improvements as well as new and principled models that either combine the two types of systems or incorporate the complementary strengths of each. Having said that, it does appear that the field is approaching the ceiling when it comes to empirical gains from new machine learning algorithms alone. Evidence for this exists in the three previous CoNLL shared tasks (from 2006 to 2008), which show that while improvements are still being made, they are rarely from the addition of new learning techniques. Does that mean that machine learning will no longer impact the field? Certainly not. For one thing most parsing systems that employ machine learning do so in a fully supervised setting using treebanks that typically come from a single or small set of domains. Leveraging semi-supervised and unsupervised learning algorithms to improve performance across all domains of written and spoken language is still an outstanding question, though some progress has been made in recent years. Furthermore, treebanks still only exist in a few languages. Leveraging treebanks from related languages to produce parsers in low resource languages is also an important problem. To do this, we will most likely require methods from semi-supervised and unsupervised learning as well as learning techniques for leveraging parallel corpora that have been developed in the statistical machine translation community.

One central problem in dependency parsing that still awaits its final solution is the treatment of non-projective dependencies. Current systems usually take one of two routes. Either they employ a parsing algorithm that can handle the complete class of dependency trees and pay a penalty in terms of rigid independence assumptions or problems of efficiency (or both), or they restrict parsing to projective structures and attempt to recover non-projective dependencies in some kind of post-processing step. Both routes achieve some level of success in capturing non-projective dependencies, but it seems that we should be able to do better by tailoring parsing algorithms to the restricted class of non-projective structures that seem to be prevalent in natural language. Ideally, we should then be able to find a better balance between the conflicting pressures of linguistic adequacy and computational complexity.

Recent years have seen an emphasis on developing parsers that are language general, which has been one of the main reasons that data-driven techniques have become so prevalent. Realistically however, there is only so far one can go with such a language agnostic approach to parser development. Languages are different, often in subtle ways, but also in drastic ways. At some point, insights from data-driven parsing will be merged back into language-specific parsers, most probably through formal grammars or other constraints. At that point, we may begin to increasingly see parsers that are both grammar-based *and* data-driven in much higher frequency than we see now. Merging the two will be trivial in some cases, but there will be many examples where a deep understanding of both the machine learning algorithms and grammar formalisms will be necessary in order to build theoretically satisfying as well as empirically practical models.

Dependency parsing has matured in the past decade. There is now a wide selection of multilingual parsers that are freely available for download. When they are combined with treebanks available in over twenty languages, we now have access to automatic parsers at a level that has never existed. Using these parsers should become more widespread. This includes parser use in standard natural language processing tasks like machine translation, lexical acquisition, and question answering, but also in related fields like information retrieval and data mining. Furthermore, using parsers to analyze the billions and billions of documents and transcripts recorded in electronic form should certainly provide insights to linguists studying the use and evolution of language. This increasing use of parsers will result in new demands and resource constraints that will further drive the questions being asked by researchers in dependency parsing.

A P P E N D I X   A

Resources

We will have a quick look at the available implementations of parsers and at treebanks. The lists we present here do not aim for completeness. Since the availability of such resources often changes, we are only trying to provide starting points.

A.1 PARSERS

For all major parsing methods discussed in chapters 3, 4, and 5, as well as for many other methods, there are implementations available. These parsers can be grouped into two classes: trainable parsers and parsers for specific languages, which normally provide a fixed combination of a parsing algorithm and a grammar. We will not provide locations for these resources since they tend to change rapidly. Interested users are advised to use their favorite search engine in order to locate these resources.

The following parsers are trainable:

- Jason Eisner's **probabilistic dependency parser** (Eisner, 1996b,a, 2000). This parser is an implementation of the grammar-based bottom-up parsing method presented in section 5.1. The parser is written in LISP.

- **MSTParser** (McDonald, 2006; McDonald, Crammer and Pereira, 2005; McDonald, Pereira, Ribarov and Hajič, 2005; McDonald and Pereira, 2006). This parser is an implementation of the graph-based parsing method presented in chapter 4. It is written in Java.

- **MaltParser** (Nivre, 2003, 2006b, 2007, 2008; Nivre and Nilsson, 2005; Nivre et al., 2004, 2007, 2006). This parser is an implementation of the transition-based parsing method presented in chapter 3. An open source version is written in Java.

- The *k*-**best Maximum Spanning Tree Dependency Parser** (Hall, 2007; Hall et al., 2007). The parser combines an arc-factored model with a maximum entropy optimizer and a reranker.

- The **Vine Parser** (Dreyer et al., 2006). This parser combines a probabilistic parser (Eisner and Smith, 2005), a probabilistic relation-labeling model, and a discriminative minimum risk reranker. The implementation is available in Dyna and C++.

- The **ISBN Dependency Parser** (Titov and Henderson, 2007a,b). This parser uses a generative history-based probability model based on Incremental Sigmoid Belief Networks. The implementation is available in C.

Parsers for specific languages include the following:

- **Minipar** (Lin, 1994, 1996, 1998a). This parser is an implementation of a principle-based parsing method for English (see section 5.3).

- The **WCDG Parser** (Foth et al., 2005; Foth and Menzel, 2005; Foth et al., 2000, 2004; Menzel and Schröder, 1998). This parser is an implementation of weighted constraint dependency parsing for German as described in section 5.2. A version for English is under construction.

- **Pro3Gres** (Schneider, 2004; Schneider et al., 2004). This parser employs a combination of chunk parsing and CYK parsing for English. The parser is written in PROLOG.

- The **Link Grammar Parser** (Lafferty et al., 1992; Sleator and Temperley, 1991, 1993). This parser is an implementation for link grammar, a variant of dependency grammar with undirected links. The parser is written in C and includes a grammar for English, but there is also a version for Russian available.

- **CaboCha** (Kudo and Matsumoto, 2002, 2000). This parser is an implementation of transition-based dependency parsing for Japanese using support vector machines.

A.2   TREEBANKS

Treebanks are used for training parsers as well as for evaluating their analyses. The available treebanks can be divided into two groups: genuine dependency treebanks and treebanks annotated in other formats for which conversions to a dependency format exist. Genuine dependency treebanks include the following:

- **Prague Arabic Dependency Treebank** (Hajič et al., 2004). This treebank is available from the Linguistic Data Consortium (LDC) for a license fee. LDC catalog no.: LDC2004T23.

- **Prague Dependency Treebank** (Czech) (Hajič et al., 2000). This treebank is annotated on 3 levels: the morphological, syntactic, and tectogrammatical level. It is available from LDC for a license fee. LDC catalog no. for version 1.0: LDC2001T10, for version 2.0: LDC2006T01.

- **Danish Dependency Treebank** (Kromann, 2003). The annotation of this treebank is based on Discontinuous Grammar (Buch-Kromann, 2005).

- **Bosque, Floresta sintá(c)tica** (Portuguese) (Afonso et al., 2002). The Portuguese treebank does not require a license.

- **METU-Sabancı Turkish Treebank** (Oflazer et al., 2003). This treebank is freely available after signing a license agreement.

A.3   DEPENDENCY PARSING WIKI

There is a wiki for dependency parsing at `http://depparse.uvt.nl/depparse-wiki/`, which collects the experience from the two CoNLL shared tasks. The wiki is a repository for parsers and treebanks, but also for best practices in the field.

Bibliography

Abney, Steven (1991). Parsing by chunks, *in* R. Berwick, S. Abney and C. Tenny (eds), *Principle-Based Parsing*, Kluwer, pp. 257–278.

Afonso, Susana, Bick, Eckhard, Haber, Renato and Santos, Diana (2002). Floresta sintá(c)tica: A treebank for Portuguese, *Proceedings of the 3rd International Conference on Language Resources and Evaluation (LREC)*, Las Palmas, Gran Canaria, pp. 1698–1703.

Attardi, Giuseppe (2006). Experiments with a multilanguage non-projective dependency parser, *Proceedings of the 10th Conference on Computational Natural Language Learning (CoNLL)*, New York, NY, pp. 166–170.

Bangalore, Srinivas and Joshi, Aravind K. (1999). Supertagging: An approach to almost parsing, *Computational Linguistics* 25(2): 237–267.

Bodirsky, Manuel, Kuhlmann, Marco and Möhl, Mathias (2005). Well-nested drawings as models of syntactic structure, *10th Conference on Formal Grammar and 9th Meeting on Mathematics of Language*, Edinburgh, Scotland.

Briscoe, Edward and Carroll, John (1993). Generalised probabilistic LR parsing of natural language (corpora) with unification-based grammars, *Computational Linguistics* 19: 25–59.

Buch-Kromann, Matthias (2005). *Discontinuous Grammar. A Model of Human Parsing and Language Acquisition*, PhD thesis, Copenhagen Business School, Copenhagen, Denmark.

Buchholz, Sabine and Marsi, Erwin (2006). CoNLL-X shared task on multilingual dependency parsing, *Proceedings of the 10th Conference on Computational Natural Language Learning (CoNLL)*, New York, NY, pp. 149–164.

Camerini, Paolo M., Fratta, Luigi and Maffioli, Francesco (1980). The k best spanning arborescences of a network, *Networks* 10(2): 91–110. DOI: 10.1002/net.3230100202

Carreras, Xavier (2007). Experiments with a higher-order projective dependency parser, *Proceedings of the CoNLL Shared Task of EMNLP-CoNLL 2007*, Prague, Czech Republic, pp. 957–961.

Carroll, John, Briscoe, Edward and Sanfilippo, Antonio (1998). Parser evaluation: A survey and a new proposal, *Proceedings of the 1st International Conference on Language Resources and Evaluation (LREC)*, Granada, Spain, pp. 447–454.

Carroll, John (ed.) (2002). *LREC 2002 Workshop Proceedings: Beyond* PARSEVAL – *Towards Improved Evaluation Measures for Parsing Systems*, Las Palmas, Gran Canaria.

Charniak, Eugene (2000). A maximum-entropy-inspired parser, *Proceedings of the First Meeting of the North American Chapter of the Association for Computational Linguistics (NAACL)*, Seattle, WA, pp. 132–139.

Chelba, Ciprian, Engle, David, Jelinek, Frederick, Jimenez, Victor, Khudanpur, Sanjeev, Mangu, Lidia, Printz, Harry, Ristad, Eric, Rosenfeld, Ronald, Stolcke, Andreas and Wu, Dekai (1997). Structure and performance of a dependency language model, *Proceedings of Eurospeech*, Vol. 5, Rhodes, Greece, pp. 2775–2778.

Cheng, Yuchang, Asahara, Masayuki and Matsumoto, Yuji (2005). Machine learning-based dependency analyzer for Chinese, *Proceedings of International Conference on Chinese Computing (ICCC)*, Bangkok, Thailand, pp. 66–73.

Chomsky, Noam (1981). *Lectures on Government and Binding*, Foris.

Chu, Y. J. and Liu, T. H. (1965). On the shortest arborescence of a directed graph, *Science Sinica* 14: 1396–1400.

Collins, Michael (1999). *Head-Driven Statistical Models for Natural Language Parsing*, PhD thesis, University of Pennsylvania.

Collins, Michael (2002). Discriminative training methods for hidden Markov models: Theory and experiments with perceptron algorithms, *Proceedings of the Conference on Empirical Methods in Natural Language Processing (EMNLP)*, Philadelphia, PA. DOI: 10.3115/1118693.1118694

Collins, Michael, Hajič, Jan, Ramshaw, Lance and Tillmann, Christoph (1999). A statistical parser for Czech, *Proceedings of the 37th Annual Meeting of the Association for Computational Linguistics (ACL)*, Collge Park, MD, pp. 505–512. DOI: 10.3115/1034678.1034754

Corston-Oliver, Simon, Aue, Antony, Duh, Kevin and Ringger, Eric (2006). Multilingual dependency parsing using Bayes point machines, *Proceedings of the Human Language Technology Conference of the NAACL, Main Conference*, New York, NY, pp. 160–167.

Covington, Michael A. (2001). A fundamental algorithm for dependency parsing, *Proceedings of the 39th Annual ACM Southeast Conference*, Athens, GA, pp. 95–102.

Crouch, Richard, Kaplan, Ronald M., King, Tracy H. and Riezler, Stefan (2002). A comparison of evaluation metrics for a broad coverage stochastic parser, *Proceedings of the LREC Workshop on the Evaluation of Parsing Systems*, Las Palmas, Gran Canaria, pp. 67–74.

Culotta, Aron and Sorensen, Jeffery (2004). Dependency tree kernels for relation extraction, *Proceedings of the 42nd Annual Meeting of the Association for Computational Linguistics (ACL)*, Barcelona, Spain, pp. 423–429. DOI: 10.3115/1218955.1219009

Daelemans, Walter and Van den Bosch, Antal (2005). *Memory-Based Language Processing*, Cambridge University Press.

Debusmann, Ralph, Duchier, Denys and Kruijff, Geert-Jan M. (2004). Extensible dependency grammar: A new methodology, *Proceedings of the COLING Workshop on Recent Advances in Dependency Grammar*, Geneva, Switzerland, pp. 78–85.

Ding, Yuan and Palmer, Martha (2004). Synchronous dependency insertion grammars: A grammar formalism for syntax based statistical MT, *Proceedings of the COLING Workshop on Recent Advances in Dependency Grammar*, Geneva, Switzerland, pp. 90–97.

Dreyer, Markus, Smith, David A. and Smith, Noah A. (2006). Vine parsing and minimum risk reranking for speed and precision, *Proceedings of the 10th Conference on Computational Natural Language Learning (CoNLL)*, New York, NY, pp. 201–205.

Duan, Xiangyu, Zhao, Jun and Xu, Bo (2007). Probabilistic parsing action models for multi-lingual dependency parsing, *Proceedings of the CoNLL Shared Task of EMNLP-CoNLL 2007*, Prague, Czech Republic, pp. 940–946.

Duchier, Denys (1999). Axiomatizing dependency parsing using set constraints, *Proceedings of the Sixth Meeting on Mathematics of Language*, Orlando, FL, pp. 115–126.

Duchier, Denys and Debusmann, Ralph (2001). Topological dependency trees: A constraint-based account of linear precedence, *Proceedings of the 39th Annual Meeting of the Association for Computational Linguistics (ACL) and the 10th Conference of the European Chapter of the ACL (EACL)*, Toulouse, France, pp. 180–187.

Earley, Jay (1970). An efficient context-free parsing algorithm, *Communications of the ACM* 13: 94–102. DOI: 10.1145/362007.362035

Edmonds, Jack (1967). Optimum branchings, *Journal of Research of the National Bureau of Standards* 71B: 233–240.

Eisner, Jason and Blatz, John (2007). Program transformations for optimization of parsing algorithms and other weighted logic programs, *Proceedings of the 11th Conference on Formal Grammar*, Dublin, Ireland, pp. 45–85.

Eisner, Jason M. (1996a). An empirical comparison of probability models for dependency grammar, *Technical Report IRCS-96-11*, Institute for Research in Cognitive Science, University of Pennsylvania.

Eisner, Jason M. (1996b). Three new probabilistic models for dependency parsing: An exploration, *Proceedings of the 16th International Conference on Computational Linguistics (COLING)*, Copenhagen, Denmark, pp. 340–345. DOI: 10.3115/992628.992688

Eisner, Jason M. (2000). Bilexical grammars and their cubic-time parsing algorithms, *in* H. Bunt and A. Nijholt (eds), *Advances in Probabilistic and Other Parsing Technologies*, Kluwer, pp. 29–62.

Eisner, Jason and Satta, Giorgio (1999). Efficient parsing for bilexical context-free grammars and head-automaton grammars, *Proceedings of the 37th Annual Meeting of the Association for Computational Linguistics (ACL)*, College Park, MD, pp. 457–464. DOI: 10.3115/1034678.1034748

Eisner, Jason and Smith, Noah (2005). Parsing with soft and hard constraints on dependency length, *Proceedings of the 9th International Workshop on Parsing Technologies (IWPT)*, Vancouver, Canada, pp. 30–41.

Foth, Kilian (1999). Tranformationsbasiertes Constraint-Parsing. Diplomarbeit, Universität Hamburg.

Foth, Kilian (2007). *Hybrid Methods of Natural Language Analysis*, Shaker.

Foth, Kilian, Daum, Michael and Menzel, Wolfgang (2004). A broad-coverage parser for German based on defeasible constraints, *Proceedings of KONVENS 2004*, Vienna, Austria, pp. 45–52.

Foth, Kilian, Daum, Michael and Menzel, Wolfgang (2005). Parsing unrestricted German text with defeasible constraints, *in* H. Christiansen, P. R. Skadhauge and J. Villadsen (eds), *Constraint Solving and Language Processing*, Springer, pp. 140–157.

Foth, Kilian and Menzel, Wolfgang (2005). Robust parsing with weighted constraints, *Natural Language Engineering* 11(1): 1–25. DOI: 10.1017/S1351324903003267

Foth, Kilian, Schröder, Ingo and Menzel, Wolfgang (2000). A transformation-based parsing technique with anytime properties, *Proceedings of the 6th International Workshop on Parsing Technologies (IWPT)*, Trento, Italy, pp. 89–100.

Gaifman, Haim (1965). Dependency systems and phrase-structure systems, *Information and Control* 8: 304–337. DOI: 10.1016/S0019-9958(65)90232-9

Georgiadis, Leonidas (2003). Arborescence optimization problems solvable by Edmonds' algorithm, *Theoretical Computer Science* 301: 427 – 437. DOI: 10.1016/S0304-3975(02)00888-5

Glover, Fred and Laguna, Manuel (1977). *Tabu Search*, Kluwer.

Haghighi, Aria, Ng, Andrew and Manning, Christopher (2005). Robust textual inference via graph matching, *Proceedings of the Human Language Technology Conference and the Conference on Empirical Methods in Natural Language Processing (HLT/EMNLP)*, Vancouver, Canada, pp. 387–394. DOI: 10.3115/1220575.1220624

Hajič, Jan, Böhmová, Alena, Hajičová, Eva and Vidová-Hladká, Barbora (2000). The Prague Dependency Treebank: A three-level annotation scenario, *in* A. Abeillé (ed.), *Treebanks: Building and Using Parsed Corpora*, Kluwer Academic Publishers.

Hajič, Jan, Smrž, Otakar, Zemánek, Petr, Šnaidauf, Jan and Beška, Emanuel (2004). Prague Arabic Dependency Treebank: Development in data and tools, *Proceedings of the NEMLAR 2004 International Conference on Arabic Language Resources and Tools*, Cairo, Egypt.

Hall, Johan, Nivre, Joakim and Nilsson, Jens (2006). Discriminative classifiers for deterministic dependency parsing, *Proceedings of the COLING/ACL 2006 Main Conference Poster Sessions*, Sydney, Australia, pp. 316–323.

Hall, Keith (2007). k-best spanning tree parsing, *Proceedings of the 45th Annual Meeting of the Association for Computational Linguistics (ACL)*, Prague, Czech Republic, pp. 392–399.

Hall, Keith, Havelka, Jiři and Smith, David A. (2007). Log-linear models of non-projective trees, k-best MST parsing and tree-ranking, *Proceedings of the 2007 Joint Conference on Empirical Methods in Natural Language Processing and Computational Natural Language Learning (EMNLP-CoNLL)*, Prague, Czech Republic, pp. 962–966.

Hall, Keith and Novák, Vaclav (2005). Corrective modeling for non-projective dependency parsing, *Proceedings of the 9th International Workshop on Parsing Technologies (IWPT)*, Vancouver, Canada, pp. 42–52.

Harper, Mary P. and Helzerman, Randall A. (1995). Extensions to constraint dependency parsing for spoken language processing, *Computer Speech and Language* 9: 187–234. DOI: 10.1006/csla.1995.0011

Harper, Mary P., Helzermann, Randall A., Zoltowski, Carla B., Yeo, Boon-Lock, Chan, Yin, Steward, Todd and Pellom, Bryan L. (1995). Implementation issues in the development of the PARSEC parser, *Software: Practice and Experience* 25: 831–862. DOI: 10.1002/spe.4380250802

Havelka, Jiři (2007). Beyond projectivity: Multilingual evaluation of constraints and measures on non-projective structures, *Proceedings of the 45th Annual Meeting of the Association for Computational Linguistics (ACL)*, Prague, Czech Republic, pp. 608–615.

Hays, David G. (1964). Dependency theory: A formalism and some observations, *Language* 40: 511–525. DOI: 10.2307/411934

Hellwig, Peter (1986). Dependency unification grammar, *Proceedings of the 11th International Conference on Computational Linguistics (COLING)*, Bonn, Germany, pp. 195–198.

Hellwig, Peter (2003). Dependency unification grammar, *in* V. Agel, L. M. Eichinger, H.-W. Eroms, P. Hellwig, H. J. Heringer and H. Lobin (eds), *Dependency and Valency*, Walter de Gruyter, pp. 593–635.

Hirakawa, Hideki (2006). Graph branch algorithm: an optimum tree search method for scored dependency graph with arc co-occurrence constraints, *Proceedings of the 21st International Conference on Computational Linguistics and the 44th Annual Meeting of the Association for Computational Linguistics*, Sydney, Australia, pp. 361–368.

Hudson, Richard A. (1984). *Word Grammar*, Blackwell.

Hudson, Richard A. (1990). *English Word Grammar*, Blackwell.

Hudson, Richard A. (2007). *Language Networks: The New Word Grammar*, Oxford University Press.

Järvinen, Timo and Tapanainen, Pasi (1998). Towards an implementable dependency grammar, *Proceedings of the Workshop on Processing of Dependency-Based Grammars (ACL-COLING)*, Montreal, Canada, pp. 1–10.

Johansson, Richard and Nugues, Pierre (2006). Investigating multilingual dependency parsing, *Proceedings of the 10th Conference on Computational Natural Language Learning (CoNLL)*, New York, NY, pp. 206–210.

Johansson, Richard and Nugues, Pierre (2007a). Extended constituent-to-dependency conversion for English, *Proceedings of NODALIDA 2007*, Tartu, Estonia.

Johansson, Richard and Nugues, Pierre (2007b). Incremental dependency parsing using online learning, *Proceedings of the CoNLL Shared Task of EMNLP-CoNLL 2007*, Prague, Czech Republic, pp. 1134–1138.

Johnson, Mark (2007). Transforming projective bilexical dependency grammars into efficiently-parseable CFGs with unfold-fold, *Proceeding of the 45th Annual Meeting of the Association of Computational Linguistics*, Prague, Czech Republic, pp. 168–175.

Kahane, Sylvain, Nasr, Alexis and Rambow, Owen (1998). Pseudo-projectivity: A polynomially parsable non-projective dependency grammar, *Proceedings of the 36th Annual Meeting of the Association for Computational Linguistics (ACL) and the 17th International Conference on Computational Linguistics (COLING)*, Montreal, Canada, pp. 646–652.

Karlsson, Fred (1990). Constraint grammar as a framework for parsing running text, *Papers Presented to the 13th International Conference on Computational Linguistics (COLING)*, Helsinki, Finland, pp. 168–173.

Karlsson, Fred, Voutilainen, Atro, Heikkilä, Juha and Anttila, Arto (eds) (1995). *Constraint Grammar: A language-independent system for parsing unrestricted text*, Mouton de Gruyter.

Klein, Dan (2005). *The Unsupervised Learning of Natural Language Structure*, PhD thesis, Stanford University.

Klein, Dan and Manning, Christopher D. (2002). Fast exact natural language parsing with a factored model, *Advances in Neural Information Processing Systems (NIPS)*, Cambridge, MA, pp. 3–10.

Klein, Dan and Manning, Christopher D. (2003). Accurate unlexicalized parsing, *Proceedings of the 41st Annual Meeting of the Association for Computational Linguistics (ACL)*, pp. 423–430. DOI: 10.3115/1075096.1075150

Koo, Terry, Globerson, Amir, Carreras, Xavier and Collins, Michael (2007). Structured prediction models via the matrix-tree theorem, *Proceedings of the 2007 Joint Conference on Empirical Methods in Natural Language Processing and Computational Natural Language Learning (EMNLP-CoNLL)*, Prague, Czech Republic, pp. 141–150.

Kromann, Matthias Trautner (2003). The Danish Dependency Treebank and the DTAG treebank tool, *Proceedings of the 2nd Workshop on Treebanks and Linguistic Theories (TLT)*, Växjö, Sweden, pp. 217–220.

Kudo, Taku and Matsumoto, Yuji (2000). Japanese dependency structure analysis based on support vector machines, *Proceedings of the Joint SIGDAT Conference on Empirical Methods in NLP and Very Large Corpora*, Hong Kong, pp. 18–25.

Kudo, Taku and Matsumoto, Yuji (2002). Japanese dependency analysis using cascaded chunking, *Proceedings of the 6th Workshop on Computational Language Learning (CoNLL)*, Taipei, Taiwan, pp. 63–69.

Kuhlmann, Marco and Möhl, Mathias (2007). Mildly context-sensitive dependency languages, *Proceedings of the 45th Annual Meeting of the Association for Computational Linguistics (ACL)*, Prague, Czech Republic, pp. 160–167.

Kuhlmann, Marco and Nivre, Joakim (2006). Mildly non-projective dependency structures, *Proceedings of the COLING/ACL 2006 Main Conference Poster Sessions*, Sydney, Australia, pp. 507–514.

Kulick, Seth, Bies, Ann, Liberman, Mark, Mandel, Mark, McDonald, Ryan, Palmer, Martha, Schein, Andrew, Ungar, Lyle, Winters, Scott and White, Pete (2004). Integrated annotation for biomedical information extraction, *Proceedings of the Workshop on Linking Biological Literature, Ontologies, and Databases (HLT-NAACL)*, Boston, MA, pp. 61–68.

Lafferty, John, Sleator, Daniel and Temperley, Davy (1992). Grammatical trigrams: A probabilistic model of link grammar, *Proceedings of the AAAI Fall Symposium on Probabilistic Approaches to Natural Language*, Cambridge, MA, pp. 89–97.

Lari, Karim and Young, Steve J. (1990). The estimation of stochastic context-free grammars using the inside-outside algorithm, *Computer Speech and Language* 4(1): 35–56. DOI: 10.1016/0885-2308(90)90022-X

Lin, Dekang (1994). PRINCIPAR – an efficient, borad-coverage, principle-based parser, *Proceedings of the 15th International Conference on Computational Linguistics (COLING)*, Kyoto, Japan, pp. 482–488.

Lin, Dekang (1995). A dependency-based method for evaluating broad-coverage parsers, *Proceedings of the Fourteenth International Joint Conference on Artificial Intelligence (IJCAI)*, Montreal, Canada, pp. 1420–1425.

Lin, Dekang (1996). Evaluation of PRINCIPAR with the SUSANNE corpus, *Robust Parsing Workshop at ESSLLI*, Prague, Czech Republic, pp. 54–69.

Lin, Dekang (1998a). Dependency-based evaluation of MINIPAR, *Proceedings of the LREC Workshop on the Evaluation of Parsing Systems*, Granada, Spain.

Lin, Dekang (1998b). A dependency-based method for evaluating broad-coverage parsers, *Journal of Natural Language Engineering* 4: 97–114.

MacWhinney, Brian (2000). *The CHILDES Project: Tools for Analyzing Talk*, Lawrence Erlbaum.

Magerman, David M. (1995). Statistical decision-tree models for parsing, *Proceedings of the 33rd Annual Meeting of the Association for Computational Linguistics (ACL)*, Cambridge, MA, pp. 276–283. DOI: 10.3115/981658.981695

Manning, Christopher D. and Schütze, Hinrichs (2000). *Foundations of Statistical Natural Language Processing*, MIT Press.

Marcus, Mitchell P., Santorini, Beatrice and Marcinkiewicz, Mary Ann (1993). Building a large annotated corpus of English: The Penn Treebank, *Computational Linguistics* 19(2): 313–330.

Marcus, Solomon (1965). Sur la notion de projectivité, *Zeitschrift für mathematische Logik und Grundlagen der Mathematik* 11: 181–192. DOI: 10.1002/malq.19650110212

Martins, André F.T., Das, Dipanjan, Smith, Noah A. and Xing, Eric P. (2008). Stacking dependency parsers, *Proceedings of the Conference on Empirical Methods in Natural Language Processing (EMNLP)*, Honolulu, Hawaii.

Maruyama, Hiroshi (1990). Structural disambiguation with constraint propagation, *Proceedings of the 28th Annual Meeting of the Association for Computational Linguistics (ACL)*, Pittsburgh, PA, pp. 31–38. DOI: 10.3115/981823.981828

McDonald, Ryan (2006). *Discriminative Learning and Spanning Tree Algorithms for Dependency Parsing*, PhD thesis, University of Pennsylvania.

McDonald, Ryan, Crammer, Koby and Pereira, Fernando (2005). Online large-margin training of dependency parsers, *Proceedings of the 43rd Annual Meeting of the Association for Computational Linguistics (ACL)*, Ann Arbor, MI, pp. 91–98. DOI: 10.3115/1219840.1219852

McDonald, Ryan, Lerman, Kevin and Pereira, Fernando (2006). Multilingual dependency analysis with a two-stage discriminative parser, *Proceedings of the 10th Conference on Computational Natural Language Learning (CoNLL)*, New York, NY, pp. 216–220.

McDonald, Ryan and Nivre, Joakim (2007). Characterizing the errors of data-driven dependency parsing models, *Proceedings of the 2007 Joint Conference on Empirical Methods in Natural Language Processing and Computational Natural Language Learning (EMNLP-CoNLL)*, Prague, Czech Republic, pp. 122–131.

McDonald, Ryan and Pereira, Fernando (2006). Online learning of approximate dependency parsing algorithms, *Proceedings of the 11th Conference of the European Chapter of the Association for Computational Linguistics (EACL)*, Trento, Italy, pp. 81–88.

McDonald, Ryan, Pereira, Fernando, Ribarov, Kiril and Hajič, Jan (2005). Non-projective dependency parsing using spanning tree algorithms, *Proceedings of the Human Language Technology Conference and the Conference on Empirical Methods in Natural Language Processing (HLT/EMNLP)*, Vancouver, Canada, pp. 523–530. DOI: 10.3115/1220575.1220641

McDonald, Ryan and Satta, Giorgio (2007). On the complexity of non-projective data-driven dependency parsing, *Proceedings of the 10th International Conference on Parsing Technologies (IWPT)*, Prague, Czech Republic, pp. 121–132.

Mel'čuk, Igor (1988). *Dependency Syntax: Theory and Practice*, State University of New York Press.

Menzel, Wolfgang and Schröder, Ingo (1998). Decision procedures for dependency parsing using graded constraints, *Proceedings of the Workshop on Processing of Dependency-Based Grammars (ACL-COLING)*, Montreal, Canada, pp. 78–87.

Milicevic, Jasmina (2006). A short guide to the Meaning-Text linguistic theory, *Journal of Koralex* 8: 187–233.

Nakagawa, Tetsuji (2007). Multilingual dependency parsing using global features, *Proceedings of the CoNLL Shared Task of EMNLP-CoNLL 2007*, Prague, Czech Republic, pp. 952–956.

Neuhaus, Peter and Bröker, Norbert (1997). The complexity of recognition of linguistically adequate dependency grammars, *Proceedings of the 35th Annual Meeting of the Association for Computational Linguistics (ACL) and the 8th Conference of the European Chapter of the Association for Computational Linguistics (EACL)*, Madrid, Spain, pp. 337–343.

Nikula, Henrik (1986). *Dependensgrammatik*, Liber.

Nivre, Joakim (2002). Two models of stochastic dependency grammar, *Technical Report 02118*, Växjö University, School of Mathematics and Systems Engineering.

Nivre, Joakim (2003). An efficient algorithm for projective dependency parsing, *Proceedings of the 8th International Workshop on Parsing Technologies (IWPT)*, Nancy, France, pp. 149–160.

Nivre, Joakim (2006a). Constraints on non-projective dependency graphs, *Proceedings of the 11th Conference of the European Chapter of the Association for Computational Linguistics (EACL)*, Trento, Italy, pp. 73–80.

Nivre, Joakim (2006b). *Inductive Dependency Parsing*, Springer.

Nivre, Joakim (2007). Incremental non-projective dependency parsing, *Proceedings of Human Language Technologies: The Annual Conference of the North American Chapter of the Association for Computational Linguistics (NAACL HLT)*, Rochester, NY, pp. 396–403.

Nivre, Joakim (2008). Algorithms for deterministic incremental dependency parsing, *Computational Linguistics* 34(4): 513—553. DOI: 10.1162/coli.07-056-R1-07-027

Nivre, Joakim, Hall, Johan, Kübler, Sandra, McDonald, Ryan, Nilsson, Jens, Riedel, Sebastian and Yuret, Deniz (2007). The CoNLL 2007 shared task on dependency parsing, *Proceedings of the CoNLL Shared Task of EMNLP-CoNLL 2007*, Prague, Czech Republic, pp. 915–932.

Nivre, Joakim, Hall, Johan and Nilsson, Jens (2004). Memory-based dependency parsing, *Proceedings of the 8th Conference on Computational Natural Language Learning (CoNLL)*, Boston, MA, pp. 49–56.

Nivre, Joakim, Hall, Johan, Nilsson, Jens, Chanev, Atanas, Eryiğit, Gülşen, Kübler, Sandra, Marinov, Svetoslav and Marsi, Erwin (2007). MaltParser: A language-independent system for data-driven dependency parsing, *Natural Language Engineering* 13: 95–135.

Nivre, Joakim, Hall, Johan, Nilsson, Jens, Eryiğit, Gülşen and Marinov, Svetoslav (2006). Labeled pseudo-projective dependency parsing with support vector machines, *Proceedings of the 10th Conference on Computational Natural Language Learning (CoNLL)*, New York, NY, pp. 221–225.

Nivre, Joakim and McDonald, Ryan (2008). Integrating graph-based and transition-based dependency parsers, *Proceedings of the 46th Annual Meeting of the Association for Computational Linguistics (ACL)*, Columbus, OH.

Nivre, Joakim and Nilsson, Jens (2005). Pseudo-projective dependency parsing, *Proceedings of the 43rd Annual Meeting of the Association for Computational Linguistics (ACL)*, Ann Arbor, MI, pp. 99–106. DOI: 10.3115/1219840.1219853

Nivre, Joakim and Scholz, Mario (2004). Deterministic dependency parsing of English text, *Proceedings of the 20th International Conference on Computational Linguistics (COLING)*, Geneva, Switzerland, pp. 64–70. DOI: 10.3115/1220355.1220365

Oflazer, Kemal, Say, Bilge, Hakkani-Tür, Dilek Zeynep and Tür, Gökhan (2003). Building a Turkish treebank, *in* A. Abeillé (ed.), *Treebanks: Building and Using Parsed Corpora*, Kluwer, pp. 261–277.

Paskin, Mark A. (2001). Cubic-time parsing and learning algorithms for grammatical bigram models, *Technical Report UCB/CSD-01-1148*, Computer Science Division, University of California Berkeley.

Paskin, Mark A. (2002). Grammatical bigrams, *Advances in Neural Information Processing Systems (NIPS)*, Vancouver, Canada.

Quirk, Chris, Menezes, Arul and Cherry, Colin (2005). Dependency treelet translation: syntactically informed phrasal SMT, *Proceedings of the 43rd Annual Meeting of the Association for Computational Linguistics (ACL)*, Ann Arbor, MI, pp. 271–279. DOI: 10.3115/1219840.1219874

Rabiner, Lawrence R. (1989). A tutorial on hidden Markov models and selected applications in speech recognition, *Proceedings of the IEEE* 77(2): 257–285. DOI: 10.1109/5.18626

Ribarov, Kiril (2004). *Automatic Building of a Dependency Tree*, PhD thesis, Charles University.

Riedel, Sebastian and Clarke, James (2006). Incremental integer linear programming for non-projective dependency parsing, *Proceedings of the Conference on Empirical Methods in Natural Language Processing (EMNLP)*, Sydney, Australia, pp. 129–137.

Sagae, Kenji and Lavie, Alon (2006). Parser combination by reparsing, *Proceedings of the Human Language Technology Conference of the NAACL, Main Conference*, New York, NY, pp. 125–132.

Schneider, Gerold (2004). Combining shallow and deep processing for a robust, fast, deep-linguistic dependency parser, *Proceedings of the ESSLLI Workshop on Combining Shallow and Deep Processing in NLP*, Nancy, France.

Schneider, Gerold, Dowdall, James and Rinaldi, Fabio (2004). A robust and hybrid deep-linguistic theory applied to large-scale parsing, *Proceedings of the COLING Worskhop on Robust Methods in the Analysis of NL Data (ROMAND)*, Geneva, Switzerland, pp. 14–23.

Schröder, Ingo (2002). *Natural Language Parsing with Graded Constraints*, PhD thesis, Hamburg University.

Schröder, Ingo, Menzel, Wolfgang, Foth, Kilian and Schulz, Michael (2000). Modeling dependency grammar with restricted constraints, *Traitement Automatique des Langues* 41(1): 113–144.

Schröder, Ingo, Pop, Horia, Menzel, Wolfgang and Foth, Kilian (2001). Learning grammar weights using genetic algorithms, *Proceedings of the International Conference on Recent Advances in Natural Language Processing (RANLP)*, Tzigov Chark, Bulgaria.

Schröder, Ingo, Pop, Horia, Menzel, Wolfgang and Foth, Kilian (2002). Learning the constraints weights of a dependency grammar using genetic algorithms, *Proceedings of the 13th International Conference on Domain Decomposition Methods (CIMNE)*, Barcelona, Spain.

Sgall, Petr, Hajičová, Eva and Panevová, Jarmila (1986). *The Meaning of the Sentence in Its Pragmatic Aspects*, Reidel.

Sleator, Daniel and Temperley, Davy (1991). Parsing English with a link grammar, *Technical Report CMU-CS-91-196*, Carnegie Mellon University, Computer Science.

Sleator, Daniel and Temperley, Davy (1993). Parsing English with a link grammar, *Proceedings of the Third International Workshop on Parsing Technologies (IWPT)*, Tilburg, The Netherlands, pp. 277–292.

Smith, David A. and Eisner, Jason (2008). Dependency parsing by belief propagation, *Proceedings of the Conference on Empirical Methods in Natural Language Processing (EMNLP)*, Honolulu, Hawaii.

Smith, David A. and Smith, Noah A. (2007). Probabilistic models of nonprojective dependency trees, *Proceedings of the 2007 Joint Conference on Empirical Methods in Natural Language Processing and Computational Natural Language Learning (EMNLP-CoNLL)*, Prague, Czech Republic, pp. 132–140.

Smith, Noah A. (2006). *Novel Estimation Methods for Unsupervised Discovery of Latent Structure in Natural Language Text*, PhD thesis, Johns Hopkins University.

Snow, Rion, Jurafsky, Dan and Ng, Andrew Y. (2005). Learning syntactic patterns for automatic hypernym discovery, *Advances in Neural Information Processing Systems (NIPS)*, Vancouver, Canada.

Starosta, Stanley (1988). *The Case for Lexicase: An Outline of Lexicase Grammatical Theory*, Pinter Publishers.

Surdeanu, Mihai, Johansson, Richard, Meyers, Adam, Màrquez, Lluís and Nivre, Joakim (2008). The CoNLL 2008 shared task on joint parsing of syntactic and semantic dependencies, *CoNLL 2008: Proceedings of the Twelfth Conference on Computational Natural Language Learning*, Manchester, England, pp. 159–177.

Tapanainen, Pasi and Järvinen, Timo (1997). A non-projective dependency parser, *Proceedings of the 5th Conference on Applied Natural Language Processing (ANLP)*, Washington, D.C., pp. 64–71.

Tarjan, Robert E. (1977). Finding optimum branchings, *Networks* 7: 25–35. DOI: 10.1002/net.3230070103

Tarvainen, Kalevi (1982). *Einführung in die Dependenzgrammatik*, Niemeyer.

Tesnière, Lucien (1959). *Éléments de syntaxe structurale*, Editions Klincksieck.

Titov, Ivan and Henderson, James (2007a). Fast and robust multilingual dependency parsing with a generative latent variable model, *Proceedings of the CoNLL Shared Task of EMNLP-CoNLL 2007*, Prague, Czech Republic, pp. 947–951.

Titov, Ivan and Henderson, James (2007b). A latent variable model for generative dependency parsing, *Proceedings of the 10th International Conference on Parsing Technologies (IWPT)*, Prague, Czech Republic, pp. 144–155.

Tutte, William T. (1984). *Graph Theory*, Cambridge University Press.

Vapnik, Vladimir N. (1995). *The Nature of Statistical Learning Theory*, Springer.

Viterbi, Andrew J. (1967). Error bounds for convolutional codes and an asymptotically optimum decoding algorithm, *IEEE Transactions on Information Theory* 13(2): 260–269. DOI: 10.1109/TIT.1967.1054010

Wallach, Hann, Sutton, Charles and McCallum, Andrew (2008). Bayesian modeling of dependency trees using hierarchical Pitman-Yor priors, *Workshop on Prior Knowledge for Text and Language Processing*, Helsinki, Finland.

Wang, Mengqiu, Smith, Noah A. and Mitamura, Teruko (2007). What is the Jeopardy Model? A quasi-synchronous grammar for QA, *Proceedings of the 2007 Joint Conference on Empirical Methods in Natural Language Processing and Computational Natural Language Learning (EMNLP-CoNLL)*, Prague, Czech Republic, pp. 22–32.

Wang, Wen and Harper, Mary (2002). The SuperARV language model: Investigating the effectiveness of tightly integrating multiple knowledge sources, *Proceedings of the Conference on Empirical Methods in Natural Language Processing (EMNLP)*, Philadelphia, PA, pp. 238–247. DOI: 10.3115/1118693.1118724

Wang, Wen and Harper, Mary P. (2004). A statistical constraint dependency grammar (CDG) parser, *Proceedings of the Workshop on Incremental Parsing: Bringing Engineering and Cognition Together (ACL)*, Barcelona, Spain, pp. 42–29.

Weber, H. J. (1997). *Dependenzgrammatik. Ein interaktives Arbeitsbuch*, Günter Narr.

Yamada, Hiroyasu and Matsumoto, Yuji (2003). Statistical dependency analysis with support vector machines, *Proceedings of the 8th International Workshop on Parsing Technologies (IWPT)*, Nancy, France, pp. 195–206.

Younger, Daniel H. (1967). Recognition and parsing of context-free languages in time n^3, *Information and Control* 10: 189–208. DOI: 10.1016/S0019-9958(67)80007-X

Yuret, Deniz (1998). *Discovery of Linguistic Relations Using Lexical Attraction*, PhD thesis, Massachusetts Institute of Technology.

Zeman, Daniel (2004). *Parsing with a Statistical Dependency Model*, PhD thesis, Charles University.

Zeman, Daniel and Žabokrtský, Zdeněk (2005). Improving parsing accuracy by combining diverse dependency parsers, *Proceedings of the 9th International Workshop on Parsing Technologies (IWPT)*, Vancouver, Canada, pp. 171–178.

Zhang, Yue and Clark, Stephen (2008). A tale of two parsers: investigating and combining graph-based and transition-based dependency parsing using beam-search, *Proceedings of the Conference on Empirical Methods in Natural Language Processing (EMNLP)*, Honolulu, Hawaii.

Author Biographies

Sandra Kübler is Assistant Professor of Computational Linguistics at Indiana University, where she has worked since 2006. She received her M.A. from the University of Trier and her Ph.D. in Computational Linguistics from the University of Tübingen. Sandra's research focuses on data-driven methods for syntactic and semantic processing. For her dissertation work, she developed a novel memory-based approach to parsing spontaneous speech. This parser was integrated into the Verbmobil speech-to-speech translation system. Sandra is currently interested in parsing German, a non-configurational language, for which several treebanks are available. Her research focuses on comparisons between constituent-based and dependency-based parsing and comparisons of how different annotation schemes influence parsing results.

Ryan McDonald is a Senior Research Scientist at Google, Inc., where he has worked since 2006. He received his B.Sc. from the University of Toronto and his Ph.D. in Computer and Information Science from the University of Pennsylvania. Ryan's research focuses on learning and inference algorithms for parsing and summarizing natural language. His dissertation work advanced the theoretical and empirical foundations for modern graph-based dependency parsers. The result of this work was the MSTParser software package, which tied for the most accurate system in the first shared task on multilingual dependency parsing at the Conference on Computational Natural Language Learning in 2006. Since arriving at Google, Ryan's research has focused on opinion mining, including methods for automatically identifying opinions, extracting relevant attributes, and building faceted summaries from large text collections.

Joakim Nivre is Professor of Computational Linguistics at Uppsala University (since 2008) and at Växjö University (since 2002). He holds a Ph.D. in General Linguistics from the University of Gothenburg and a Ph.D. in Computer Science from Växjö University. Joakim's research focuses on data-driven methods for natural language processing, in particular for syntactic and semantic analysis. He is one of the main developers of the transition-based approach to data-driven dependency parsing, described in his 2006 book *Inductive Dependency Parsing* and implemented in the MaltParser system. Systems developed using MaltParser were tied for first place in the shared tasks on multilingual dependency parsing at the Conference on Computational Natural Language Learning in both 2006 and 2007. Joakim's current research interests include the analysis of mildly non-projective dependency structures, the integration of morphological and syntactic processing for richly inflected languages, and the modeling of human sentence processing.

Printed in the United States
by Baker & Taylor Publisher Services